The Man Who Hated Sherlock Holmes

A man of action, a giant of a man, Sir Arthur Conan Doyle was a heavyweight boxer, a top-ranking cricketer, a Rugby forward, a golfer, and a pioneer skier.

He served aboard a whaler in the Arctic, then aboard a cargo and passenger ship along the west coast of Africa, where he nearly died of tropical fever. He was a doctor who practiced successfully in the south of England, then studied in Vienna and set up as an eye surgeon in London. He served England in three wars:

He wrote magnificent historical novels about medieval and Puritan England and about the Napoleonic wars. He wrote successful plays, books expounding his belief in spiritualism, and multivolume histories of the two wars in which he participated most actively.

And, though he sometimes regretted it, he perfected the modern detective story and created the most famous detective who ever followed a clue. So well did Sir Arthur Conan Doyle succeed in this that Sherlock Holmes and his trusted companion, Dr. John H. Watson, have very nearly thrown into shadow Conan Doyle himself and the many accomplishments he considered far more important than the infallible detective.

In this account of Conan Doyle's extraordinary life and work, James Playsted Wood gives us a full portrait of a man as fascinating and nearly as astonishing as his own most celebrated creation, the hawk-nosed Holmes.

Pantheon Books

A Life of Sir Arthur Conan Doyle

The Man Who Hated Sherlock Holmes

By

James Playsted Wood

Illustrated by Richard M. Powers

for E.C.W.

The Man Who Hated Sherlock Holmes

1

Born in Scotland of Irish parents, descended from the valiant Percies of Northumberland and the Plantagenet kings of England, he was a giant of a man. He was a heavyweight boxer, a top-ranking cricketer, a football player, a golfer, and an expert billiards player. A man of action, surging with unquenchable vitality, he introduced skiing into Switzerland and drove his own car, a Dietrich-Lorraine, in international competitions.

He served aboard a whaler in the Arctic, then aboard a combined cargo and passenger ship along the west coast of Africa, where he nearly died of tropical fever. He was a doctor who, after early adventures in medicine and some years of successful practice in the south of England, studied in Vienna and set up practice as an eye surgeon in London.

He served England in three wars. He was a correspondent in the Egyptian Sudan, a doctor in action with the British forces in South Africa during the Boer War, a private of the Volunteers and, in the uniform of a deputy lieutenant of Surrey, a front-line observer during World War I.

He wrote magnificent historical novels about medieval and Puritan England, about the Huguenots in France and New France, and about the Napoleonic wars. He wrote realistic medical stories and sensational tales of adventure. He wrote successful plays, prophetic science fiction, stirring verse, distinctive literary appreciation, books about spiritualism, and multivolume histories of the two wars in which he participated most actively.

Sir Arthur Conan Doyle perfected the modern detective story and created the most famous detective who ever followed a clue. So well did he succeed that Sherlock Holmes and his trusted companion and Boswellian biographer, Dr. John H. Watson, are so famous and still so much alive that they have very nearly thrown into shadow all else that Dr. A. Conan Doyle (he preferred the earned title of his profession to that of the knighthood bestowed on him by Edward VII in 1902) was and accomplished.

Arthur Conan Doyle was born in Edinburgh, May 22,

1859, one of the ten children of Charles Altamont Doyle and Mary Foley Doyle. His father was an artist. All three of his uncles, his father's brothers, were artists. Like Sherlock Holmes, the boy had art in his blood.

His grandfather, John Doyle, of an old Anglo-Irish family, had gone from Dublin to London where he became rich and famous as a political caricaturist. He was tall, stately, and commanding, resembling the great Duke of Wellington who had defeated Napoleon at Waterloo.

One of this John Doyle's sons, Richard Doyle, was a well-known illustrator for *Punch*, the English magazine of wit and humor, whose familiar cover he had designed. Another son, James Doyle, compiled the *Official Baronage* of England and wrote and illustrated *The Chronicles of England*. A third son, Henry Doyle, was a painter and an expert on painting and director of the National Gallery in Dublin.

The fourth son, Arthur Conan Doyle's father, was the youngest and the least successful. An architect as well as a painter, Charles Doyle was employed in the government's Office of Works in Edinburgh. His salary was small and never increased greatly. Sensitive and retiring, a devout Roman Catholic, as were all the Doyles, he preferred to give away his paintings rather than face the pain of possible rejection when he attempted to sell them.

Doyle's mother, who had been educated in France, was round-faced, vivacious, five feet one inch tall. She was the daughter of a doctor of Trinity College. Through her mother, Katherine Pack, she proudly traced her ancestry back more than five hundred years. It was through his mother that Arthur Conan Doyle was descended from the Percies who had several times intermarried with the Plantagenets of England's royal house. In Paris a great-uncle, Michael Conan, who was also the boy's godfather, traced his descent from the dukes of Brittany, several of whom were Conans.

Noble and even royal blood flowed in the Doyles of Edinburgh, but they had little money. Gifted Charles Altamont Doyle was not equipped to compete. He was gentle, ineffectual, and defeated. It was his wife who made ragged ends meet and who dominated the household and her son's boyhood.

Energy and common sense combined with studiousness and incurable romanticism in the tiny woman, short-sighted and growing plump, who, Doyle says, was always the great lady, whether she was bargaining with the butcher or breaking in a new houseworker. She stirred porridge with one hand while she held the *Revue des Deux Mondes* in the other and eagerly scanned its pages. She read as she knitted, read as she scrubbed. There was a family legend that while she was simultaneously reading and feeding one of the babies, the infant turned its head and, without noticing, she spooned porridge into its ear.

Mary Foley Doyle kept up with the best French authors of the day — Gautier, the Goncourts, Flaubert — but her real passion was genealogy, family history, the glorious past, particularly the past of the Packs. Her pride in her family was matched by her delight in the medieval panoply of feudalism, her love of heraldry, and her thorough belief in the ideals of knighthood which she drilled into her favorite. She made the heroes of romance and the greatness of his knightly ancestors as real to the boy as the people and facts of daily life about him.

By the time he was a schoolboy under a pock-marked, switch-wielding master in an Edinburgh school, Arthur Conan Doyle had other heroes as well. Mayne Reid was his favorite author, and he read the thrillers written by this Irishman, who had adventured all over the American frontier and served at the storming of Chapultepec in the war between the United States and Mexico, as fast as the books appeared or he could get his hands on them. *Boy Hunters*, *The Rifle Rangers*, *The Bush Boys*, *The Boy Tar*, *The War Trail* — he read them all. *The Scalp Hunters* was his favorite.

American influence reached Arthur Conan Doyle early. Visions of ambushes, buffalo hunts, encounters with bears, wolves, and mountain lions, with redskins in war paint, danced in his head. He thrilled to hairbreadth escapes in the Rockies or on the western plains. These places were as familiar to him as King Arthur's court and the grey streets of Edinburgh.

Adventure and the wide open spaces. These were for him. He loved a good story, the more sensational the better. Manly conflict in the great outdoors, sports or war: it was this which stirred the imagination of the muscular and stalwart but highly impressionable boy. Whether it was Indians and settlers banging away at each other or knights and bowmen having at the enemies of England made little difference.

He tried to emulate his heroes on the Edinburgh streets. His companions were boys as rough and ready as he. Arthur Conan Doyle at eight or nine years of age was always in the forefront of their fights with even rougher boys. Then and always he liked to fight, but chivalry having been instilled in him by his mother, he always chose as his opponents boys who were as big as or bigger than he, never smaller victims. Once he chose nobly but unwisely. Using either superior strategy or the weapon nearest at hand, a bootmaker's boy bounced a green baize bag with a boot in it on Doyle's skull and knocked him senseless. Robert Louis Stevenson, nine years older than Doyle, lived in a more polite section of Edinburgh.

There were warriors behind Arthur Conan Doyle, but there were artists as well. Art as well as fire flowed in his blue blood. Undoubtedly the boy inherited some of the artistic sense and impulses of his London grandfather and some of the talent which his father expressed in painting elves and fairies and sometimes in more powerful and even brutal work. Certainly he must have inherited his mother's quick intelligence, just as he got from her the love of books, the habit of constant reading, and all she could teach him of heraldic shields and badges and coats of arms. The small boy grew up seeing bright pennons flying, lances gleaming in the sun — a few Kentucky rifles and coonskin caps among them — and knights on war horses, a lady's favor in every shining helmet, charging to single combat for glory, honor, and the sheer fun of it.

Like most British boys of good family, Doyle was early sent away from home to school. Like most of them, he went with a show of fearlessness and wept for fright and loneliness. At ten he entered Hodder, a school in Lancaster in the north of England, to prepare for nearby Stonyhurst, a Jesuit public school. Except for six weeks each summer, he spent two years at Hodder. He had a new hero now. Sir Walter Scott joined Mayne Reid in appeal. There was a set of Scott in dark green bindings in the Picardy Place house in Edinburgh. Doyle had owned the novels long before he could read and understand them. When he could, he realized what a priceless treasure he had. He read and reread the Waverley novels, read them in the dead of night by the light of candle ends, a sense of crime, he remembered in later years, adding zest to the stories.

Of all of Scott, *Ivanhoe* was his favorite. He devoured *Ivanhoe*, reading it until he must practically have memorized its pages. Hodder seemed not so bad when it was peopled by Wilfred of Ivanhoe, the Lady Rowena, the beautiful dark Rebecca, Robin Hood, Friar Tuck, with the villainous Sir Brian de Bois-Guilbert foiled at every turn by Ivanhoe and Richard the Lionhearted himself. The school playground resounded to the trumpets and clanging steel of the great tournament at Ashby-de-la-Zouche, and grubby schoolboys were knights in shining armor.

It was a disaster when Doyle dropped his first copy of *Ivanhoe* into a stream, to find it three days later, water-soaked, swollen, and ruined. *Quentin Durward*, which he also loved, could not quite take its place. He soon managed to get another copy of *Ivanhoe*.

Stonyhurst was a huge medieval dwelling which had been left to the black-robed Jesuit priests about one hundred and fifty years before Doyle entered. The medieval curriculum still prevailed. With his fellows, Doyle studied Latin, Greek, poetry, rhetoric, grammar, and mathematics. The standards of the school were high. The Jesuits were severe masters but just, and Doyle had to measure up. The regime was strict and the school diet plain but healthy. Breakfast was dry bread and hot watered milk. There was a joint of roast meat and pudding twice a week at dinner. For supper at night there was bread, butter, potatoes, and hot milk. In the afternoon there was bread and something that passed for beer.

Discipline was severe at Stonyhurst, and punishment for wrongdoing or infraction of any of the school's rules was swift, sure, and painful. It was at least nine blows, usually twice that number, on the hand with a piece of India rubber about the size and shape of the sole of a heavy boot. One blow, Doyle says, would swell and discolor the hand. Twice nine blows made it impossible for the culprit to turn the handle of the door and escape the torture chamber. It was a point of honor, of course, not to cry out.

Doyle was beaten more often than most of his fellows. He was not particularly unruly, but he would not be forced. Restriction or the threat of violence always caused him to rebel. He emulated the manliness and hardihood he had learned from the unflinching heroes of Mayne Reid and Sir Walter Scott.

Merely an average student at first, Doyle became a

better one, excelling in English composition. The writing of assigned verse, a hopeless task for most of the students, came naturally to him and gave him a pleasure he could not yet understand. In time he became editor of the Stonyhurst magazine. Even then he was no angel. In answer to a question, he told an inquiring priest that he planned to become a civil engineer. The priest smiled gently and admitted that he might someday be an engineer but he did not think he would ever be a very civil one.

An athlete from the first, Doyle gloried in cricket, Rugby, swimming, and hockey. He did his assigned studies, but felt he learned more from what he picked up almost by accident. Mathematics, he was as convinced in later life as when he was a schoolboy, did him no good at all. He got more from good translations of the classics than from enforced study of Greek and Latin. He learned the art of reading aloud while reading to his mother as she knitted. He learned French from the adventure stories of Jules Verne. When his Paris uncle, Michael Conan, sent him a copy of the *Lays of Ancient Rome* by Thomas Babington Lord Macaulay, he learned even more on his own.

Macaulay was a revelation to Conan Doyle. Macaulay delighted him as did Reid and Scott, but differently. It was the sweep and roll of the sonorous lines as well as the color and action of the verse stories that stirred him. Macaulay's *Essays*, when he read them, delighted him still further. This became the book from which he drew the most pleasure and profit now. Looking back long

afterward, Doyle said that the *Essays* seemed entwined with his whole life. The sentences entranced the Stonyhurst boy. They rang in his ears like strong chords of solemn music.

When he was sixteen he spent two weeks of the Christmas holidays of 1874 with his Doyle relatives in London. As soon as he had reached the great city and checked his bags, telling no one, he hurried to Westminster Abbey and paid his homage at Macaulay's grave.

The London visit was a brilliant success. Arthur Conan Doyle was made much of by his respected and well-to-do uncles and aunts in their comfortable and well-appointed homes. He went to the theater, to the zoo, to Madame Tussaud's famous waxworks where, prophetically, he was particularly fascinated by the Chamber of Horrors with its frightening dramatic wax figures of famous murderers and their unhappy prey.

When Doyle returned to Stonyhurst it was to the fearsome ordeal of final examinations in Latin, Greek, French, English language and history, and mathematics. He had to pass all of them in order to sit for the matriculation — or entrance — examinations for the University of London. He passed the school examinations comfortably, and then amazed everyone, but mostly himself, by taking honors in the London examinations. One result was that Stonyhurst wrote his mother promising to remit all of her son's school fees if he were dedicated to the Church, that is, trained for the priesthood. Mrs. Doyle refused, and Doyle decided that both the Church and he had had a narrow escape. The Jesuits then offered to send Conan Doyle for another year of preparatory schooling to a Jesuit school in the Vorarlberg province of Austria so that he could learn German.

Thus it was to Feldkirch that Doyle traveled the next year, 1875. Discipline was gentler at Feldkirch. The food was better than at Stonyhurst, and the German beer was much better. Doyle did not learn much German, for he associated mostly with the other English and Irish boys at the school, but football was fun and the tobogganing was wonderful. Best of all, perhaps, was the huge horn he played in the school's brass band. It was so enormous that it took the biggest student to hold it upright.

He discovered another author too. This time it was Edgar Allan Poe. Poe, often credited with inventing the short story, could send shivers up and down your spine. Doyle dived into "The Gold Bug," "The Pit and the Pendulum," "The Murders in the Rue Morgue," "The Fall of the House of Usher," "The Masque of the Red Death." Inspired anew, Doyle sent copies of humorous verse of his own and stories he wrote for the Feldkirch paper to his uncle Michael Conan.

Poe was really something to tootle your horn about. One day Doyle blew into it until his bulging cheeks turned blue and his eyes began to pop out. He managed to get a blurred burble and a thin squeak out of it, but that was all. His fellow bandsmen had stuffed all his sheets and blankets into the horn.

2

He had seen London. When his year at Feldkirch was over, Doyle saw Paris on his way home from Austria. There he spent several happy weeks with his Uncle Michael, whom he found as rapt a student of family history and heraldry as his mother. His godfather had been favorably impressed by his writing and was certain that his tall seventeen-year-old nephew had talent. This thrilled Doyle almost as much as his first sight of France.

He had been away from home at Hodder, Stonyhurst, and Feldkirch for seven years. Now he was returning to

Scotland for very different studies. Aided and abetted by Dr. Bryan Charles Waller, his family had decided that he would enter the University of Edinburgh to study medicine. Arthur Doyle did not mind. The picture of himself in a black frock coat and a tall hat with his stethoscope tucked inside it going about healing the sick rather appealed. He felt sure he could win a scholarship which would defray a large part of his university expenses.

Soon after he reached home he took the examination and won the scholarship, or bursary as it was called in Edinburgh. Then, through some clerical error, the scholarship was awarded to someone else, and he was forced to depend on his family and on what money he could earn for the five years of his medical studies.

Like any other medical student of the time, he studied botany, physiology, chemistry, anatomy, and many more compulsory subjects, some of which he felt bore little relation to the medical art. Perhaps he was right, but everything that Doyle studied, everything he read, his associations with his fellows, the eccentricities of his professors, what he observed in hospital wards and operating theaters was to be useful to the young man when he found what his real profession was.

Doyle was not an outstanding student at Edinburgh. He won no academic distinctions. He was always, he says, a sixty-per-cent man at examinations. There were at least two good reasons for this.

One reason was that he allowed himself only a few pennies for lunch. Usually he spent these on a mutton pie and a glass of beer. As Doyle puts it, his big body won. Sometimes it did not. There was a secondhand bookshop nearby with tubs of old books outside priced at threepence each. About one day a week, his mind won, and Conan Doyle went hungry to buy copies of Tacitus, Addison, Swift, Pope, Clarendon's *History*, a life of Francis Bacon, and other treasures which he could not resist. Reading was a passion which the fired imagination in the big medical student could not still. Medicine had to share his mind with literature. Boxing, his favorite exercise, and Rugby, in which he played forward, kept his body fit and hard.

There was a harder reason for Doyle's comparatively low marks. To earn badly needed money, he compressed the work of each academic year into half that time so that he could work during the other six months as a medical assistant to doctors already established in practice. He advertised for such posts in the medical journals, and the first he got was an assistantship to a Dr. Richardson in one of the poorer sections of Sheffield, a manufacturing city in Yorkshire in England. The job lasted just three weeks. Doyle and his employer could not get along. While he waited for answers to a new advertisement, Doyle went again to London where once more he stayed with his important relatives for a few weeks. From London he went as assistant to a Dr. Eliot in a small town in Shropshire.

When classes began again at the University, he watched one of his teachers with amazed curiosity. Dr. Joseph Bell, a surgeon at the Edinburgh Infirmary, was gaunt

and dark, a wiry man with a thin, high-nosed face and penetrating grey eyes. He was famous for the swiftness and accuracy with which he could find out what was wrong with a patient. Seemingly he could tell at a glance not only what the man or woman was suffering from, but also, from dress, bearing, muscular development, or a telltale callus on the hand, in what trade or profession the patient was engaged.

For some reason Dr. Bell took a fancy to the big Conan Doyle and made him his outpatient clerk. This meant that Doyle had to question the patients, find out who they were and what their complaints were, before he ushered them one by one into the consulting room where Dr. Bell sat grandly behind his desk surrounded by students and assistants. It startled Doyle, as it astounded the others, to find out how often Dr. Bell's deductions jibed with the information he had already elicited from the patients.

When once more he was free of classes, Doyle went as an assistant to Dr. Reginald Ratcliffe, a well-known medical practitioner in the busy city of Birmingham in the industrial Midlands of England. Dr. Ratcliffe, who had a five-horse city practice — that is, he kept five horses busy making his rounds — took in fees amounting to about 3,000 pounds a year (then equal to about $15,000), a very large income at the time. Though a hard task-master, he was a friendly and genial man. He used his assistant to make up prescriptions, to assist in cases of childbirth, and to look after minor cases. The pay was small, but the doctor and his pleasant wife treated Doyle almost as a son. When he had finished another year at the University, Doyle returned to Birmingham and the Rat-cliffes, and then again for a third stay.

This was his life when Conan Doyle, who could never be busy enough, wrote his first published and paid-for work. In the spring of 1879 he wrote "The Mystery of Sasassa Valley." The short story was accepted by *Chambers's Journal* and published that October. Doyle was overjoyed. He dashed off more tales. Most of them were rejected. Like other beginning authors, Doyle quickly knew the dejection following rejections, then the delight of the occasional acceptance which spurs the aspiring author on to try again.

When later he sold "Bones" and "The Gully of Blue-mansdyke" to *London Society*, he felt he had discovered a profitable avocation. These first stories were imitative of still another American author's work. Doyle had been reading the realistic but sentimental mining-camp stories of the very popular Californian Bret Harte, who was now United States consul in Glasgow. Harte's best-known stories were "The Luck of Roaring Camp," "Tennessee's Partner," and "The Outcasts of Poker Flat." Harte's influence on Doyle was strong and lasting.

Charles Altamont Doyle, health and spirit broken, was now in a convalescent home. The son realized that his father had been thrown into a life environment which he had not been strong enough to face. Charles Doyle died a few years later.

In 1880 Arthur Conan Doyle embarked on the first of his adventures at sea. He sailed as ship's surgeon aboard the whaling ship *Hope*, bound for seven months in the Arctic. It was an eye-opening and wildly invigorating experience for the medical student who had all but finished his course, and Doyle reveled in it. There were fifty men in the crew, about half of them Scots, the other half from the Shetland Islands. The first mate was a weak little man. The cook's assistant was a giant with a red beard. As soon as the *Hope* was at sea, they happily changed places.

It was a rough, hard life with hard, rough men. Doyle soon found that his chief job was to be a companion to the *Hope's* captain, John Gray, a skipper he liked and admired, but Doyle was not content with this. The purpose of the long, lonely voyage was the hunt, the tracking down and killing of valuable seals and whales, and Doyle was soon in the thick of it. It was sport on a scale he had never dreamed of.

The *Hope* soon found the seal pack. A great slaughter ensued, the ice and snow running with blood. Twice on the first day of the kill Doyle was tossed into the icy sea by the high-running swells. Twice he was hauled out with his frozen clothes as hard as a suit of armor. After the men had killed all the seals they could bag, the *Hope* went on for whales. She had eight boats, each manned by harpooner, steerer, and oarsmen. Doyle went in the eighth with a redheaded Highlander manning the harpoon gun, a swarthy outlaw for coxswain, the steward, the second engineer, and the donkey-engine operator and himself as crew. Harpooning the whale, then lancing him to death was exciting and dangerous sport. Doyle

gloried in it. The *Hope* caught four whales, a great haul.

Doyle did his share of the hunting and killing, boxed with the men, and was fascinated by the Arctic. For those seven long months the crew of the whaler were without news or letters, completely out of touch with civilization. There was no other vessel within eight hundred miles. The deep blue of the water, the dazzling glare of the ice, the everlasting daylight, the crisp, dry air exhilarated him. It was intoxication just to be alive in such a place with such men as sailed the *Hope*. Doyle boarded the whaler an overgrown youth. He came off it, he says, a well-grown and powerful man. The superb physical health he knew all his life and the inexhaustible energy which enabled him to attempt and accomplish so much he attributed to this Arctic adventure.

Conan Doyle was paid fifty pounds for the voyage, the largest sum of money he had yet earned. His fellows liked him as well as he liked them. Men always responded to Doyle. Captain Gray offered double the salary if he would make a second voyage on the *Hope*. Though he was fascinated, Doyle refused.

He returned to Edinburgh in August 1881, took his degree as a Bachelor of Medicine and Master of Surgery, then went to sea again. This time he sailed as ship's doctor on the *Mayumba* of the African Steam Navigation Company, bound for the west coast of Africa. He was hired to look after the health of twenty or thirty passengers, but he found again that his chief duty as a ship's officer was to be a companion to the captain. It was gentleman's duty in a navy blue uniform with brass buttons, on a ship which called at many ports to discharge cargo and pick up palm nuts and oil, ivory, and other products of what was then "the Dark Continent."

Delayed by heavy storms, which gave the new young doctor plenty of very seasick passengers to tend, the *Mayumba* called first at Freetown, the capital of Sierra Leone, then at Monrovia, capital of Liberia. The tropics provided none of the stimulation Doyle had found in the Arctic. The African coastline was a monotony of blazing sun on burning sand against which shone the white line of the breaking surf. Doyle thought it a region of disease and death, unfit for white men. He was soon looking after fever-stricken patients.

At Lagos, Doyle himself came down with tropical fever. There was no ship's doctor to look after the doctor. For days he burned and tossed in his bunk. A passenger who had been stricken at the same time died. Stronger Conan Doyle recovered shakily. Soon his great strength reasserted itself and, after stops at Fernando Po and Victoria, he recovered enough to paddle a canoe through the dark and fetid jungle swamps.

Life aboard the *Mayumba* was luxurious. It was too easy, too enervating, too soft a berth, Conan Doyle decided, for a young man who had his way to make in the world. One year of such self-indulgence was fine. Two might well make him lazy and worthless. He made up his mind that he would cease his wanderings and go back to work.

It was a rough voyage home. The *Mayumba* caught fire between Madeira and England. She finally docked at Liverpool late in January 1882, and Conan Doyle went home to face a serious crisis.

While a student at the University of Edinburgh, he had begun to have religious doubts. It was hard for him to believe anything which could not be proved logically. He liked the beauty and the traditions of organized Christianity. He thought the Church useful as a guide to the unthinking and uneducated, but he rebelled against many of its doctrines. Renouncing the Roman Catholic Church or any church, he became an agnostic — one who believes that the real nature of God and the universe cannot be known.

Conan Doyle was never an atheist. Never for one instant, he says, did he doubt or deny the existence of God. But he just would not accept any belief which could not be proved to him.

His mother was not shocked. She had changed somewhat in her allegiance, and she left the Roman Catholic Church for the Church of England. It was a different matter with the strictly devout Doyles in London. They wrote, suggesting that Conan Doyle come to London to discuss his prospects in life with them. The Doyle family were in a position to obtain medical posts for their talented nephew or to help send a large and lucrative practice his way. They were anxious to help a young Catholic doctor.

When Conan Doyle told them frankly and honestly about his religious doubts and insisted on the right to follow the dictates of his own mind and conscience, they changed their minds. They offered no help, and Doyle knew that he could not expect preferment or favorable influence from them. Help came instead from an unusual and unexpected source.

At the University, Doyle had been friendly with another medical student, a ferocious Rugby forward. The son of a well-known doctor, he was a muscular, deep-chested, square-shouldered, black-headed bundle of fury with intense blue eyes and a voice and laugh like a bull. He intended to return to his home and take over his father's practice, but he was full of other world-shattering plans as well — plans for a new and impenetrable armor plate for battleships, for torpedoes, and for starting a newspaper. Boisterous, reckless, clever, genial, and vindictive by turns, he seemed capable of anything.

Doyle, who calls his friend "James Cullingworth" in *The Stark-Munro Letters*, visited him once at the other's request after they had obtained their degrees. He found him and his shy and timid but worshipful little wife virtually starving in a huge, unfurnished house which was besieged by creditors. Cullingworth first tried to borrow money. Doyle had none to lend. The other then determined to start practice in some other city where he would not be overwhelmed by his father's reputation or be seeking patients among people who had known him as a small boy. At Doyle's suggestion he called his creditors together and promised that if they would cease dunning him, he would repay them in full as soon as he was established elsewhere. His creditors agreed, and Cullingworth vanished.

Now he began to bombard Conan Doyle with excited

telegrams which urged him to join him in a fabulously successful practice in Plymouth, a port city on the south coast of England.

Despite his mother's protests, for Mary Doyle disliked and distrusted his friend, Doyle packed his bags and went. He was astounded at what he found. Cullingworth and his wife had an even larger house now, but it was far from empty. It was jammed with patients. So was his stable. So was his courtyard, and the doctor and his wife were taking in money faster than they could count it.

Roaring with triumphant laughter, Cullingworth boasted that he was hated for good reason by every other doctor in the city. He had taken all their patients. He could not possibly see all the patients who flocked to beseech his aid. He needed Doyle's help.

Cullingworth had hit upon a marvelous scheme. He charged his patients nothing for consultation. He charged them thoroughly for the drugs which he prescribed. He bullied his patients, rushed them roughly through his crowded office, ordered huge doses of medicine, signaling his frantically busy wife how much to charge each time for the prescriptions she made up. The patients loved it. So did Cullingworth for the fortune it was bringing him. He was working miracles by what Conan Doyle saw as a mixture of personal magnetism and judicious poisoning.

Cullingworth set Doyle up with a brass plate bearing his name with the word "Surgeon" on the outside of the house, and a table and a few chairs in a room inside. The mob came to see Cullingworth, but a few were diverted and sought the new doctor. A steady trickle came to Doyle from the first. He even traveled upcountry and cut a skin cancer from the nose of an old man who had smoked a short pipe under it so long that the tip had become infected. He left him, he says, with an aristocratic and almost supercilious nose.

Exulting noisily in his spectacular success, Cullingworth exploded with grandiose plans for greater and grander ventures of all kinds. He merely laughed when Doyle asked him whether he had paid off his old creditors. This, when she heard of it, disgusted Doyle's honest mother, who wrote him describing in no uncertain terms what she thought of a man capable of such conduct. Doyle defended his friend in letters back. His mother was not to be mollified. She felt that her wellborn son demeaned himself by this base association and cried out that James Cullingworth was even more unscrupulous than she had thought.

The Cullingworths and Doyle had a riotous time, and then they didn't. The noisy enthusiasm, roaring laughter, and magnificent promises would suddenly stop. Cullingworth, who had been beaming, would look at Doyle suspiciously and his dutiful wife coldly. Then the uproar was on again. The promises grew larger and the schemes more ridiculous. Busy with his patients, applying all he had learned in Edinburgh and learning more of medicine as he practiced, Doyle paid little attention to these inexplicable changes of mood.

Suddenly Cullingworth announced that Conan Doyle would have to leave. His presence, he claimed, was upsetting the patients. They came expecting to see one doctor, and when they saw the name of a second doctor on the plate and saw him at work in the same house, they were put off. Doyle, who thought he had been doing well and had noticed no falling off in the crowds who swarmed to the house, was astounded and hurt.

What he did not know was that Cullingworth and his wife had been reading the letters from his mother which, carelessly, he left in the office jacket which he hung on a convenient peg when he went out. The Cullingworths did not explain, for they planned a savory revenge.

Cullingworth now suggested that Doyle leave Plymouth and set up on his own in some other city. To make the start easy for him, he promised that he would give Conan Doyle a pound a week until he was well established in a new practice. It was not a large amount, but it was enough to get by on until fees began to come in.

The offer seemed generous enough, and Doyle felt he had earned it through his efforts in Plymouth. Though he was surprised at the turn events had taken, he pried his brass plate from the house, packed his bags, and set off for Portsmouth. He chose Portsmouth because it was another port which he felt might provide much the same class of practice as Plymouth.

Portsmouth, England's chief naval base, is made up of Landport, Portsea, and Southsea, the resort section of the city to the southeast. It was a thriving city with a population of about 150,000 when Conan Doyle went there. It had its great shipyards and dockyards, with the protecting fortifications which made it a garrison as well as a naval town. It had fine old houses and churches and already a literary tradition. His father a clerk in the dockyards, Charles Dickens had been born in Landport in 1812. It was to Southsea, with its esplanade, its castle built by Henry VIII, and its naval monuments and memorials, including the anchor of Lord Nelson's flagship, the *Victory*, that Conan Doyle made his way.

Big as he was and as seasoned a traveler, a doctor with varied experience already behind him, Doyle must have had a few butterflies in his stomach when he landed with his professional name plate, a small leather trunk, and a hatbox on the railway station platform in Portsmouth. For one thing, he had only five pounds and eighteen shillings in his pocket or anywhere else in the world. He had no friends in a strange city. His prospects were shakily uncertain.

A friendly streetcar conductor helped him with advice as to where he might find centrally located lodgings and dropped him at what Doyle saw as a shabby-genteel kind of thoroughfare. He rented a clean bedroom-sitting room for thirteen shillings a week, then went back to the Portsmouth station for his luggage. In the evening he strolled the nearby streets. It was a pleasant evening, the air soft and sweet. A military band was playing in the park. Doyle decided that he liked the city he had come to conquer. A few moments later he was not so sure.

Under a street lamp a crowd had gathered to watch a drunken scissors grinder beat his wife. Abuse of any woman was something Doyle could not stand. He intervened. Before he knew it, he had lost his stick and had his hat batted down over his ears. Then he took a hard blow on the throat and the world spun off axis for a moment. When his opponent bored in swinging, head down, Doyle nearly cracked his knuckles over the man's hard skull.

Conan Doyle was near disaster, and he knew it — not from the man's blows but from the whole episode. His dignity is as precious to a twenty-three-year-old doctor intending to set up practice in a new place as his medical diploma. A sailor saved him. Pitching into the fray, he asked for and received all the murderous attention of the drunk, and Conan Doyle, a little battered, slipped thankfully away.

Very quickly Doyle set about finding a house that would be suitable for both a home and a doctor's office. He found one, an eight-room house on a busy street between a church and a hotel. The well-to-do quarter of the town was on one side of the house, a poorer quarter on the other. The brick house in Bush Villas, Elm Grove, Southsea, was an ideal location for a new doctor.

The rent was reasonable, forty pounds a year. It came to fifty pounds with taxes. The rub was that it was customary to pay a quarter of a year's rent in advance, and Doyle did not have the money. By giving Cullingworth, on whose promised one pound a week he relied, and his uncle Henry Doyle in Dublin as references, he was able to take possession without the customary advance, and the house agent handed over the key.

It delighted Conan Doyle to have a house of his own

for the first time in his life. After cleaning up the place, he spent four pounds, almost his entire remaining capital, on secondhand (he says it may well have been tenth-hand) furniture. This got him a table, three chairs, and a patch of carpet for a front room that he fitted up as an office and consulting room for patients. He nailed up a few pictures, hung some dark brown curtains. At least one room of his eight was furnished.

He had bought an old iron bedstead. He made a wash-stand of an old packing case he found in the yard. These made up the furnishings of his upstairs bedroom. A back room he rigged up as combined kitchen and dining room. In it he had a stool and his trunk, which served inside as a storage bin for his food and outside as a table to eat from. There was a gas jet on the wall. Doyle devised an extension to this which enabled him to boil water for his tea and to fry his bacon. He became expert at slicing bacon so thin that he got a marvelous number of strips from a pound. Tea, bread, bacon, and an occasional fish became his spare diet — and he thrived on it.

Drugs he got on credit. He got ten more badly needed pounds by writing the editor of *London Society*, asking for an advance on future work and selling him "My Friend the Murderer."

Now he wrote Cullingworth telling him that he had obligated himself for a year's rent and spent about all the money he had and could obtain, but saying he felt sure that with the promised pound a week he could easily survive until patients began coming in. A reply came quickly, and Doyle opened Cullingworth's letter with the excited expectation that it would contain his remittance.

It did not. Instead it contained a fiery letter denouncing him. A maid, the letter said, had cleared some torn bits of paper from the fireplace of the room he had had at Plymouth. Thinking it might be something of importance which should be sent on, Mrs. Cullingworth had pasted the bits together and found that they made up a letter from Doyle's mother which denounced Cullingworth as a bankrupt swindler and described him in other uncomplimentary terms. The Cullingworths professed to be amazed that, while he was a guest in their house, Doyle should have been a party to such a correspondence. Not only would the promised money not be sent, but also they wished to have nothing more to do with him.

Doyle was taken aback. He had incurred the responsibilities of his house and the other expenses of setting up in practice on the strength of Cullingworth's promise. He was angered and disbelieving. Then he remembered something. He had never destroyed one of his mother's letters. All of them were still in his pocket. He knew that the Cullingworths had extracted the letters from his jacket and read them. This, then, accounted for their changing moods, their alternating pleasant and unfriendly attitudes.

Suddenly the absurdity of the situation struck him. The picture of the Cullingworths carefully raking the bits of torn paper from the sooty fireplace and pasting together scraps of a letter that was still intact in his pocket was too much for Conan Doyle. Despite his predicament, he burst into laughter.

Doyle could not afford a maid or any household help. Under cover of darkness he polished his own brass plate and swept down his outer hall and street steps. More and more people stopped during the day to read his sign. Just enough came in to keep him going. Some could not pay. A gypsy woman with a sick child not only could not pay, but also left with the gift of a few small coins that the doctor could ill afford. Others who strayed in paid enough to keep him in tea and bacon. While he waited for more profitable patients, Doyle passed the time by writing more stories.

London Society was paying him an average of four pounds, or about twenty dollars, for each story now. He got other stories into *All the Year Round, Temple Bar, The Boys' Own Paper*, and other of the lesser popular magazines that published thrillers.

His spirits were high. He liked Southsea with its parks, the mineral well that made it a popular resort and watering place, and the beautiful countryside surrounding it. He was making friends, as Conan Doyle always made friends, and he was in exuberant health. His spirits were so high that at night, when all hope of patients had gone, he would lock his house and stride for miles to work off his energy.

The house was growing more comfortable. His mother sent him sheets, blankets, pictures, books, even a tea cosy. One of his London aunts shipped him more furniture and decorations. Soon his mother sent him something else, his small brother Inness, an alert ten-year-old whom Doyle found a bright and merry companion. Inness, with the brass buttons of a page on his jacket, answered the door and ushered in the patients, sometimes with an involuntary cheer when the sight of one promised a few shillings and pence that they needed for groceries. He became the young doctor's younger companion on his nighttime walks.

Inness had only one vice. He liked to cut out paper soldiers or buy toy lead soldiers when he could get his hands on a few pennies. Dr. Doyle was sometimes embarrassed by having to sweep a regiment of foot soldiers or a troop of cavalry from his consulting-room table before he could reach out to take a patient's pulse.

One other gift Dr. Doyle refused. One of his uncles sent him a letter of introduction to the Bishop of Portsmouth who he said he was sure would be glad to help a struggling young Catholic doctor. Doyle did not use the letter. He still insisted on his right to think independently. He would have refused the introduction had it come from some eminent Protestant soliciting the help of the Protestant community. In fact, in *The Stark-Munro Letters*, in which Doyle tells of his early days as a doctor in the form of letters from "Dr. Stark Munro" in England to "Herbert Swanborough" in Lowell, Massachusetts, he describes the introduction as coming from a titled uncle who was an ardent Methodist, or Wesleyan, addressed to an old friend who was the chief Methodist minister of "Birchespool."

Dr. Stark Munro also gave his American friend, who

had been a fellow medical student, some sound practical advice based on his Southsea experiences.

Do not think that practice will come to you. You must go to it. You may sit upon your consulting room chair till it breaks under you, but ... you will make little ... progress. The way to do it is to get out, to mix everywhere with men, let them know you. ... A noisy smoking concert where you will meet eighty men is better for you than the patient or two whom you might have seen at home. ...

You must inspire respect. Be friendly, genial, convivial — what you will — but preserve the tone and bearing of a gentleman. ... Above everything, beware of drink! ... I do not mean merely festive societies. Literary, debating, political, social, athletic. ... You must throw yourself into each with energy and conviction. You will soon find yourself on the committee — possibly the secretary, or even in the presidential chair. ... These are the rungs up which one climbs.

In Portsmouth, Conan Doyle joined everything in sight. He became a familiar and popular, tall and broad-shouldered figure in literary and political clubs and in sports. If a patient came while he was playing cricket, and playing almost like a professional, Inness gravely told the man or woman that the doctor was engaged, then slipped around to the playing field and brought his big brother home.

Doyle's planned gregariousness paid off. He worked his practice up to 154 pounds the first year in Southsea, to 250 the second year. Encouraged, he was inspired with an idea which would make life more comfortable for Inness and him and improve their social status. Through a newspaper advertisement, he let the basement floor of the house and two upstairs rooms to two elderly women, who purported to be sisters, in exchange for cooking, housekeeping, and tending the door.

For a time everything went beautifully and the brothers relaxed in comparative luxury. Doyle even ventured to "lay down a cellar" consisting of one cask of beer. Soon the seaman husband of one of the supposedly unmarried women turned up. Then it turned out that the women were not sisters at all but merely friends. Then noisy quarrels broke out below stairs. Finally the quieter and more efficient of the two women tearfully announced that she could stand it no longer and left. At her suggestion, Doyle investigated his cellar and found that his cask of beer was empty.

Conan Doyle immediately dismissed the other woman, her husband, and their mongrel dogs. The trouble was, as Doyle says, that he and Inness had been demoralized by luxury. He sought out the blameless woman, paid her eleven shillings for the small stock of matches, shoelaces, shoe polish, and penny candles with which she had set up shop in a poorer quarter of the town, and then installed her as their sole housekeeper. The new arrangement worked perfectly.

In addition to what his general practice brought in, Dr. Doyle had a small but steady income from examining applicants for life insurance. He was earning an additional ten to fifteen pounds a year by writing tales for the popular magazines. It was thrillers he had delighted in as a boy. It was thrillers he had made up and told his schoolfellows at Hodder and Stonyhurst. It was thrillers he wrote now, sensational stories charged with action, breath-catching suspense, dark mysteries, cliff-hanging climaxes. Many of these were set in distant lands he had never seen. Doyle was a born storyteller from the first.

One day in March 1885 a medical colleague called Dr. Doyle in for a consultation. As soon as he saw Jack Hawkins, severely ill and mentally disordered from cerebral meningitis, Doyle knew that the consultation was a mere formality. The case was hopeless. Hawkins was the son of a widow who had brought him and her young daughter to stay in Southsea. The immediate need was for lodgings where the patient could be cared for. No hotel or boardinghouse would take him, and his family shuddered at the idea of his being confined in a sanitorium. By agreement with the other physician, Doyle fitted up a room in his own house where the sometimes convulsive and violent patient would be comfortable and could have immediate medical attention when it was needed.

Despite Doyle's care and the constant attendance of his mother and of his gentle, blue-eyed, brown-haired sister, Jack Hawkins grew worse. Early one morning he escaped from bed half-crazed and smashed most that was breakable in his room. One night soon afterward he seemed so bad that Conan Doyle called in his colleague to see if he could suggest any measures not yet taken. The next day young Hawkins died.

Doyle had been drawn to the pretty, grief-stricken sister. As circumstances brought them together under emotional strain, friendship became love. Doyle's mother, who had been visiting him, thoroughly approved of "Touie." Doyle and Louise Hawkins were married August 9, 1885.

Inness went off to a public school in Yorkshire where, after the death of her husband, Doyle's mother also lived. Touie and Mrs. Hawkins, together with the housekeeper, became the Southsea household. Only after his marriage did Doyle discover that his wife had an income of one hundred pounds a year of her own. He did not pretend to be displeased.

Marriage delighted him. Almost unnoticed, Inness and he had fallen into unconventional and careless ways. His marriage changed all that. His home now was neat, bright, and comfortable. His wife became his beloved companion. Doyle's aroused emotions sharpened his wits and gave new meaning to life. They stimulated his writing, and he began to attempt work of a higher order.

The Cornhill Magazine, of which Thackeray had been founding editor and to which Arnold, Ruskin, Trollope, and Stevenson had all contributed, paid him thirty pounds for "Habakuk Jephson's Statement." This was double the amount he had earned for all his output for the lesser magazines in a year. He wrote more stories for James Payne, editor of *The Cornhill*, and broke into *Blackwood's Edinburgh Magazine* with "The Physiologist's Wife," a triangular love story. *Blackwood's*, founded in 1817, is still the best magazine of adventure narratives in English. Decidedly, *The Cornhill* and *Blackwood's* were several steps up from *The Boys' Own Paper*.

Dr. Conan Doyle's income from his medical practice rose now to some three hundred pounds a year, but he was beginning to taste success and obtain financial reward from his pen. Writing became more and more important to him, and his medical interests slipped gradually into second place. Most of the magazines did not give the names of the authors of their stories. Only a few readers knew who had written them. Doyle knew that he would not become known as an author until his name appeared on the title page of a successful book. Ambitiously, he began a novel, *The Firm of Girdlestone*.

When it was finished, Doyle sent it immediately to a publisher. It came back rejected. He submitted it to other publishers. It came back again and again. No publisher would take it. Doyle did not blame them. He knew it was a poor book.

Instead of growing despondent, he began searching for fresher and more colorful material. He remembered Poe's detective, M. Dupin. He knew the writings of the French novelist Emile Gaboriau, who had pioneered in detective fiction twenty-odd years before. A detective story might be just the thing. But what kind of a detective? Doyle remembered, too, Dr. Joseph Bell, whose outpatient clerk he had been in medical school, and how his sharp eyes and acute observation took in telling details at a glance and enabled him to make startlingly accurate deductions from what he saw. Suppose he had a trained detective, eagle-faced and hawk-eyed like Bell, able to reduce this deductive talent to a science! The idea began to take shape.

Doyle needed a name for his hero. He thought first of names like "Fox" or "Sharp," but soon discarded any which in the fashion of caricature were obvious character tags. He settled finally on the monosyllabic, easily remembered "Holmes," with its pleasant sound and its association with "home." For a given name he needed something a little more distinctive. Some names seemed too commonplace, others too precious. Finally he chose "Sherlock." The name was familiar to him through his reading of Macaulay, for a William Sherlock had been dean of St. Paul's Cathedral in the seventeenth century. He may also have liked its closeness to "Sherwood," with its suggestion of Sherwood Forest, Robin Hood, and the Sheriff of Nottingham.

Doyle knew that Sherlock Holmes would have to have a companion, an intelligent but more ordinary individual, an educated man of action, who could participate in and tell about the exploits of his hero. He knew a Dr. James Watson. "Watson" was the kind of ordinary name that would do. Holmes's companion might well be a doctor; Doyle knew doctors. He changed the given name of his friend and gave him a middle initial. "Dr. John H. Watson" became the shadow of the great Sherlock Holmes.

Very quickly, through Dr. Watson, Dr. A. Conan Doyle told the first Holmes adventure, *A Study in Scar-*

let. He sent it immediately to James Payne of *The Cornhill.*

Payne kept the manuscript about a month and then sent it back. *A Study in Scarlet* was too long for a short story, too short for a book that could be serialized in a magazine. Payne did not say so, but he may also have thought the story too sensational for his conservative publication.

Doyle sent the manuscript to another publisher. It came back unread. A third publisher finally said that he could not publish it as a book, for the market was flooded with cheap fiction that year, but if Doyle would accept twenty-five pounds for the complete rights, he would hold it for a year, then publish it as one of a collection of stories. As this was the best as well as the only offer he had received, Doyle agreed. *A Study in Scarlet* was published in *Beeton's Christmas Annual* for 1887, and the public met Sherlock Holmes and Dr. Watson for the first time.

3

Dr. A. Conan Doyle did not wait to see how his brain children fared. He was already far too deeply immersed in what he considered a much more important and worthwhile job of writing. He thought of Sherlock Holmes as a deliberately created device, a kind of exaggerated Dr. Joseph Bell working with criminal rather than with medical symptoms. *A Study in Scarlet* was merely an ingenious tale. Its overly long second part, set in the American West, owed as much to the sensationalism of Mayne Reid as to the melodramatics of Bret Harte, and he must have known this. He did not know that in Holmes and Watson he had introduced two of the most fascinating and durable characters in English fiction.

Far more important to him right now than the machinations of a London detective as reported by a credulous physician was the brave and stirring history of England and the novel that he was trying to fashion out of a stern part of it.

The colorful and dramatic past had been vivid to Doyle from childhood. First his mother, then Sir Walter Scott and Lord Macaulay, had made it as real for him as the events he lived through himself. Doyle saw history always in terms of action, adventure, and story — in terms of strong and brave men fighting for England, honor, and the sport of the fight. He poured his own zest for living into the figures of the past, his own love of sport and of masculine courage and daring.

In the seventeenth century, England suffered the turmoil and bloodshed of bitter civil wars. These broke out in Scotland, then ravished all England and Ireland. Two questions, one civil and one religious, were in dispute. King James I insisted on his divine right to rule as he pleased, regardless of the wishes of the people as expressed through Parliament. He also insisted that everyone worship according to the forms of the Church of England. Those who sided with the king were the Royalists or Cavaliers. Those who opposed him and gathered around Oliver Cromwell, who became their leader, were the Puritans or Roundheads.

The first civil war broke out between these forces in

1642. The Puritans under Cromwell defeated the Royalists. King Charles I, who had succeeded his father in 1625, was captured in 1646 and tried and beheaded in 1649. The Puritans set up a government called the Commonwealth, which ruled England without a king. From 1653 to his death in 1658, Oliver Cromwell ruled the Commonwealth as Lord Protector of the realm. In 1660 the Commonwealth was dissolved and England's monarchy restored under Charles II, son of the executed Charles I, who returned from exile in France to rule until his death in 1685. James II, a Catholic king, succeeded him.

Conan Doyle, who admired the sturdy Roundhead warriors who had fought under Oliver Cromwell, opens his story at this point. Perhaps his own religious experience had heightened his sympathy with these earlier rebels. Certainly the force and strength of his own character made him feel at one with the robust Puritans who had fought under "Old Ironsides," as Cromwell was called, for what they considered their rights.

In 1685 a Protestant conspiracy was afoot to unseat James II and replace him on the throne of England with the exiled Duke of Monmouth, a son of Charles II, who had been smuggled back into England by his Puritan followers. It is the story of this rebellion that Doyle tells through Micah Clarke, who purportedly is telling the story to his grandchildren.

Micah was the giant son of Colonel Ironside Joe Clarke, one of Cromwell's valiant warriors. Born in Hampshire in 1664, he was a youth of twenty when he and a companion, Reuben Lockarby, fished the incredible Decimus Saxon out of the waters of the Solent, which is the channel between the Isle of Wight and the English mainland.

A big man, Doyle liked to write of other big, lusty young men like Micah Clarke. Decimus was an old and tried campaigner, a wily soldier of fortune and an astute judge of character, including his own, who was also an expert with the rapier, the broadsword, or with any weapon. As Sherlock Holmes had Dr. Watson for foil, Micah had the sturdy but more dully colored Reuben Lockarby. These three companions set out to join Monmouth's forces. On the way they are joined by a fourth. Sir Gervas Jerome, young, handsome, foppish, reckless, gallant, is careless of what side he fights on so long as he fights. These are typical Doyle characters — a strong and vital youth with a more prosaic companion, a cunning older warrior, and a noble and dashing wit — all of them as brave as bravery and as honorable as honor.

Typical, too, is Doyle's manner of telling his spirited tale. Doyle liked to have one character tell the story. This use of the first-person narrative convinces the reader of the truth of the story. It also makes it impossible for the author to tell what all but one of the characters thinks and feels, for the narrator cannot read the minds and emotions of his companions. Thus the author can get on with the story — with the action, the fire and color which seldom slow in a Doyle story.

Doyle spent months in reading and research to prepare for the writing of *Micah Clarke*. He knew accurately the time, the scene, and the people. It was Doyle's habit to know what he was talking about. Not until he was thoroughly familiar with late seventeenth-century England did he start to write. Then he wrote *Micah Clarke* rapidly. This was his way of working. He spent his time on thorough preparation and on the working out of plots. Then when he came to sit down and write he could write almost without pause.

Micah, Decimus, Reuben, and the nonchalantly gallant Gervas pick up followers as they journey toward Taunton, Puritan meeting place of the adherents of Monmouth. All England of 1685 passes before the reader. Doyle gets in all the life and color of the road. There are skirmishes, man-to-man fights, tests of strength and valor. He gets in all the piety and fire of the Puritan peasants rising against the well-armed soldiery of the king with battered swords, scythes, sickles, flails, and even stones.

At Taunton the rabble they have gathered becomes Colonel Saxon's Regiment of Wiltshire Foot with Micah, Reuben, and Sir Gervas each commanding companies under Decimus, who proves himself a stern and battle-hardened drillmaster. Sterner still and more inflexible of purpose is Master Timewell, Taunton's ancient mayor. Doyle could draw character after the Dickens manner of giving individual traits to strongly marked types of men and women. At Taunton the Duke of Monmouth was proclaimed King of England.

On July 6, 1685, the Puritan force of about three thousand men attacked the much larger and better-armed forces of King James at Sedgemoor, near Bridgewater.

Doyle's account of the battle is vivid. Micah and his companions suffer differing fates. Doyle describes the terrible aftermath of the rebellion as vividly as the battle scenes. *Micah Clarke*, romantic in conception and treatment, is painstaking in its profuse detail, realistic and even brutal in some of its episodes. It is a fine historical novel that has long been a well-loved boys' book.

Dr. A. Conan Doyle knew that he had written well. Publishers to whom he submitted the newly finished manuscript were not so sure. Some were certain that he had not. James Payne of *The Cornhill* said Doyle was wasting his time writing historical novels. A newspaper syndicate rejected the book. *Blackwood's* rejected it. Publisher after publisher sent the manuscript, read or unread, back to its author in Southsea. Not until after almost a year of trial did Doyle send the manuscript to Longmans. Fortunately this publishing house gave the worn packet to Andrew Lang to read. Lang was a Scottish scholar and prolific journalist, best known now for his many collections of fairy tales.

Andrew Lang enthused about *Micah Clarke*, and Longmans accepted it for publication.

Near the end of January 1889 the Doyles' first child was born. The girl was named after both Doyle's mother and his wife. She became Mary Louise Conan Doyle. In February *Micah Clarke* was published, and its favorable reception by the critics vindicated Dr. Doyle's high opinion of his work. Then and later he viewed *Micah Clarke* as his first solid literary achievement, calling it the cornerstone on which his reputation was built.

His historical novels mattered greatly to Conan Doyle, yet it was for more stories about Sherlock Holmes that he was asked. Ward, Locke and Company, which had issued a separate edition of *A Study in Scarlet* in 1888, were the London publishers of *Lippincott's Magazine* of Philadelphia. This was one of the better American magazines of its day. It had published Oscar Wilde's *The Picture of Dorian Gray* and Kipling's *The Light That Failed* as well as works by American writers, including Henry James, Frank R. Stockton, Sidney Lanier, and William Gilmore Simms. On a visit to London the magazine's editor asked Conan Doyle for more stories about Sherlock Holmes.

In Philadelphia, J. B. Lippincott published an American edition of *A Study in Scarlet* in 1890. In the February 1890 issue of *Lippincott's Magazine* it ran complete in twelve chapters "a new novel by A. Conan Doyle," *The Sign of the Four; or, The Problem of the Sholtos.* The story, which opened the issue, took up almost half its pages, the only other substantial piece being an article by Julian Hawthorne on how his father, Nathaniel Hawthorne, wrote his books and stories. James Whitcomb Riley, Agnes Repplier, Bert Harte, Lafcadio Hearn, and Owen Wister all wrote for *Lippincott's* in 1890. Dr. A. Conan Doyle, Sherlock Holmes, and Dr. John H. Watson made their American debut in good company.

Not far from Portsmouth is the New Forest. It is "new" only because certain other of England's royal forests, like the Forest of Dean in Gloucestershire, are older. New Forest was set aside as a royal hunting preserve by William the Conqueror in 1079.

With several other doctors from the Portsmouth Eye Hospital, Doyle spent a few days there during the Easter holidays of 1889. He returned alone with as many books about the Middle Ages in England as he could find and, in part of a scene that he intended to use, began to work up the background for a second historical novel.

Doyle had been bred on the age of chivalry. He believed implicitly in the knightly creed of truth and honor, the seeking for glory, the fight for the right, and the tournament tests of manhood. Like Miniver Cheevy in Edwin Arlington Robinson's poem, though for different reasons, he loved "the medieval grace of iron clothing." He set out to put the time of Edward III on paper, not as it appeared in 1889 but as it had actually been in 1366. He had ready for his pen all the heraldic lore taught him unforgettably by his intent mother. He had new rich material and skills gathered during his mature years.

Arthur Conan Doyle was a doctor. A doctor is present at birth and often at death. He knows life between at close hand. When a doctor is sensitive and imaginative and accustomed to dealing with people's emotions as well as with their physical health, he has a cumulative knowledge and wisdom that few other men can have.

There have been many great writers in English who were doctors. Sir Thomas Browne, who wrote *Religio Medici,* the religion of a doctor, in 1643, was a physician. The nineteenth-century romantic poet John Keats was educated to be a surgeon. One of Doyle's literary heroes, Oliver Wendell Holmes, was both a doctor and a professor in the Harvard Medical School. In Philadelphia, S. Weir Mitchell was a famed neurologist as well as a popular historical novelist. Somerset Maugham was a doctor trained in St. Thomas's Hospital in London. Sir William Osler, the Canadian whose *Principles and Practice of Medicine* is a medical classic, was an accomplished writer as well as a famed physician. Robert Bridges, England's Poet Laureate from 1913 to his death in 1930, was a doctor of medicine.

A. Conan Doyle shared experiences and talent with men like these. As a young assistant in Birmingham, as a surgeon in Plymouth and a general practitioner in Southsea, he had tended men of all sorts and conditions. He knew men and women in joy and in grief, well or dying. He knew that human nature changes little from century to century. He also knew that life in medieval times was far different from what it is in modern times.

Doyle knew one more thing that fitted him to write all his books, whether detective fiction or historical romance. He knew how to read a book and extract from it the information he wanted. As a medical student he had had to familiarize himself with many subjects, and the habit of study and his developed skill in extracting lore from books enabled him to delve fruitfully into history of many kinds. His writer's skill enabled him to select from what he found and to present what he wished in words that made the past live again.

Doyle used all these abilities and called all his basic

character and temperament into play when he wrote books like *Micah Clarke* and now *The White Company*. The whole man was vibrantly alive as he worked. Undoubtedly this is one reason why these books always seemed to him the best and most important of all his writing.

On the second Thursday after the Feast of the Assumption a novice of the holy monastic order of the Cistercians was brought up before the abbot of Beaulieu on charges. The year was 1366. The charges were that Hordle John, a giant of a youth, had drained a quart pot of beer intended for four of the novices. When Brother Ambrose remonstrated, Hordle John held the unhappy brother face downward over a fishpond for as long as it pleased him. He was also seen to speak with the daughter of a forester. For these crimes Hordle John was stripped of his habit and thrust into the outer world.

The next day another youth left Beaulieu. In contrast to bull-like Hordle John, he was slight, handsome, and wellborn. Since infancy twenty years before he had been sheltered in the abbey and taught all that the monks could teach him. Now, in accordance with the abbot's promise to his father, Edric the Franklin, it is time for Alleyne Edricson to go forth.

Brawn and brain join when Alleyne and Hordle John meet on the road. They share adventures with jugglers, bailiffs, thieves, and wandering musicians. At a country inn, the Pied Merlin, they meet Samkin Aylward, a bowman veteran of the wars in France who is recruiting men to serve there with the famed White Company. The toughened soldier of fortune has now made his appearance. When they unite in service under Sir Nigel Loring of Castle Twynham, Doyle's cast of leading characters is complete.

Sir Nigel is no Walter Scott hero. He is forty-six, undersized, stooping, and blind in one eye. He is also lithe as a tiger, brave as a lion, and as fanatically devoted to the knightly code as only a Doyle hero can be. His sight had been injured in battle. Sir Nigel tells how. "It was a woman's hand which cast this lime into mine eyes, and though I saw her stoop, and might well have stopped her ere she threw, I deemed it unworthy of my knighthood to hinder or balk one of her sex."

Alleyne sets forth as Sir Nigel's squire while Hordle John serves in the ranks under Aylward. For a lady's token Alleyne carries the green veil of Sir Nigel's daughter, Maude, who will marry him if he serves her father well and acquits himself in battle as becomes the man of her choice. There is plenty of opportunity to "worshipfully gain worship" in *The White Company*. Its pages roll with broad humor, flame with ardor, ring with exaltation as the steel-helmeted archers of England and her mounted knights seek out her massed enemies in France and Spain.

As imaginative authors do, Doyle came to know his characters and their world better than he knew Portsmouth and his patients or even, perhaps, his wife and small daughter. He rejoiced with bald, soft-spoken Sir Nigel, swaggering Aylward, honest Hordle John, and glory-smitten Alleyne. He lived their story, gloried in their triumphs, suffered their wounds, echoed their patriotism, and swore by their knightly code.

Doyle cultivated a simple style in the book. He avoided long words and wrote so clearly and so smoothly he was afraid that the flow of the story hid the amount of scholarship he built into his book. No matter; once more he was certain of the worth of what he wrought. When he finished *The White Company*, he let out an exultant shout and flung his pen across the room, splashing ink on the wall. He was sure that some day everyone who could read English would know the heroes of his tale and glory in their story. So fond was he of the whole that when his son was born a few years later, he named him Alleyne — Alleyne Kingsley Doyle — after the young knight in shining armor whom he had created.

James Payne, who had rejected both *A Study in Scarlet* and *Micah Clarke*, enthusiastically accepted *The White Company* for *The Cornhill*. Arrangements were speedily made for its publication in book form, and Conan Doyle looked for new worlds to conquer.

Restlessly, he set out for Berlin where a Dr. Koch advertised that he would demonstrate a new and certain cure for tuberculosis. When he got there, Doyle was uncivilly treated and refused admission to the demonstration. Infuriated and disbelieving in the validity of the Koch cure after he had studied it, he wrote a letter to the *Daily Telegraph* in which he attacked the cure which, he felt, only aroused false hopes in the victims of tuberculosis and their families.

The trip to Germany only whetted his strong ambitions. He was dissatisfied now with Southsea where he had been successful as both doctor and writer. For some time he had been interested in the eye. He decided to study abroad and, when he returned to England, set up as an eye specialist. He knew that he could study as well in England, but he also knew the advertising value to a specialist of residence and work abroad.

Dr. Doyle relinquished his Portsmouth practice, gave up his home, and in December 1890 left with his wife and small daughter for Vienna. For four months he attended lectures on the eye at the Krankenhaus, mingled socially with other English residents, enjoyed the ice skating, and wrote a small book, *The Doings of Raffles Haw*, to help defray expenses. After a visit to Paris on the way back to England, the Doyles went to London, where they engaged lodgings in Montague Place, off Russell Square near the British Museum.

For 120 pounds a year, Doyle rented a front room and the use of part of a waiting room at 2 Devonshire Place for his quarters as an eye specialist. This was at the top of Wimpole Street and just off Harley Street, where London's fashionable physicians had their consulting rooms. Dr. Doyle hoped that his nearness to them and his new shingle as an oculist would attract patients and that the general medical practitioners would refer patients with eye ailments to him.

In this he was disappointed — but not too greatly disappointed. His real interest now was his writing, not his profession. He already had an idea for a new historical novel and was gathering his materials for a tale of the Huguenots, the French Protestants driven from France by the revocation of the Edict of Nantes, which had guaranteed them religious toleration.

It was a story of these people who emigrated from France to New France in Canada that Doyle decided to write. Neither his strategic location nor his neighboring physicians were turning him trade. His office made instead an ideal place to plan and write *The Refugees, A Tale of Two Continents.*

Every morning, clad in the frock coat and top hat that were the badge of his profession, Doyle walked sedately from his lodgings to his office, getting there about ten o'clock in the morning. He studied, reflected, and wrote until three or four o'clock in the afternoon, then, as befitted an oculist with offices near Harley Street, walked sedately back to his lodgings with the fruits of his day's work on the sheets of paper in his pocket.

Not one single patient ever interfered with this delightful routine, but Sherlock Holmes and Dr. John H. Watson of 221 B, Baker Street did.

A new popular magazine had appeared, *The Strand.* Doyle wrote a new Sherlock Holmes story for it, and it was accepted. As both *A Study in Scarlet* and *The Sign of the Four* had been small books, "A Scandal in Bohemia" was actually the first Holmes short story. Doyle promptly wrote five more Holmes stories for *The Strand:* "The Red-headed League," "A Case of Identity,"

"The Boscombe Valley Mystery," "The Five Orange Pips," and "The Man With the Twisted Lip." All were promptly accepted and published.

The stories were illustrated by Sidney Paget, who drew the lean, sharp-featured, gimlet-eyed Sherlock Holmes in his deerstalker cap and Inverness cape, the curved pipe hanging from his mouth, familiar ever since. Perhaps it was the illustrations. Perhaps it was the short-story form. Perhaps it was the popularity of *The Strand*. Perhaps it was Doyle's more incisive writing, his clever plots, and his sharp character drawing. Probably it was a combination of all of these and other factors which are difficult to isolate which led to the sudden, startling, and enthusiastic reception of Sherlock Holmes.

There were no movies. There was no radio. There was no television. The stage, novels, and short stories were the universal entertainment. A novel or a fictional character appearing month after month in complete stories that yet formed part of a continuing series could achieve the popularity now heaped on actors, animated cartoon characters, professional athletes, and photogenic politicians. Sherlock Holmes did.

Conan Doyle had been building a solid reputation as a historical novelist. His name had been on the way to becoming well known. Suddenly, and through the popularity of what he considered one of his lesser creations, he was gratifyingly, almost disconcertingly, famous.

The Strand knew when it had a good thing. When any magazine editor finds that a feature has caught on, built up the circulation of his paper, and increased the demand for copies, he cannot rest until he is sure he can get more of the same thing. *The Strand* asked Conan Doyle for more Sherlock Holmes stories.

Conan Doyle refused. He had come to a new turning point in his career. His practice as an oculist had been almost as spectacular a failure as his Sherlock Holmes was a success. By August 1891 Dr. Doyle's record was unblemished. He had still not had one patient. Instead he had had a bad attack of influenza. It had killed his sister Annette, and almost killed him. He was as weak and as emotional as a child, but his mind seemed clearer than it had ever been.

All he had been doing was wasting the earnings from his pen to keep up an oculist's rooms which no one but he ever entered. He would do it no more. He would abandon medicine and trust to his writing. In his autobiography Doyle describes the wild rush of joy he felt in reaching the decision. He was still in bed. He picked up a handkerchief from the coverlet and tried weakly to toss it to the ceiling.

The Doyles moved now to larger quarters. They found a modest house in the London suburbs at 12 Tennison Road, South Norwood, and Doyle planned to settle down to the writing of *The Refugees*. He had still to delay, for *The Strand* was pressing frantically for more Sherlock Holmes.

Finally, advancing his price to fifty pounds for each adventure, Conan Doyle agreed to write six more of the Sherlock Holmes stories. He wrote them rapidly, for he wanted them out of the way of his more serious work.

"The Adventure of the Blue Carbuncle" and "The Adventure of the Speckled Band" he wrote in one week of October 1891. Working from eight in the morning until noon, then from five to eight in the evening, he soon finished the remaining four: "The Adventure of the Engineer's Thumb," "The Adventure of the Noble Bachelor," "The Adventure of the Beryl Coronet," and "The Adventure of the Copper Beeches." All of the *Strand* stories appeared in book form in both London and New York in 1893 as *Adventures of Sherlock Holmes*.

Freed of his nonexistent practice, established once more in a comfortable home of his own where his sister Lottie lived with them and his son, Alleyne Kingsley, was born, Doyle seemed to explode into action. He was exhilarated by success. He was sought after. He met other well-known writers of the day and became the close friend of James M. Barrie, the diminutive Scots author and successful playwright whose *Peter Pan*, not yet written, was to become a children's classic. The association with Barrie inspired him to attempt a new form. He transformed one of his stories, "A Straggler of '15," a tale about a heroic old soldier of the Napoleonic wars, into a one-act play titled *Waterloo* and sent it to the great actor, Henry Irving. Irving was delighted with it, put it into his repertory, and played it for many years.

Doyle then plunged into writing *The Refugees* and promised a publisher a short novel about Napoleon.

Sherlock Holmes had other plans for him.

4

A bookseller on lower Fourth Avenue in New York
City, a section of Manhattan known for many years for
its old bookshops, offered enthusiastically to sell me
copies of the lives of Sherlock Holmes and Dr. John H.
Watson. He knew them. He had read all about them.
He had a dozen books about them. He had calls for them
all the time. When I told him that what I really wanted
was a copy of a particular book about Sir Arthur Conan
Doyle that I had been unable to find in other shops or in
the libraries, he shook his head. He didn't know of any
books at all about anyone by that name.

When, somewhat incredulous, I tried to explain that both Sherlock Holmes and Dr. Watson were creatures of Doyle's imagination and that, real as they were, they had never actually existed in the flesh, he told me flatly that I was wrong. When I protested, he did not contradict me again, for after all I was a potential, if weirdly mistaken, customer. He simply looked pityingly at me and renewed his offer to supply me with biographies of Holmes and Watson and all kinds of stories about them. He knew I would like them. Everybody liked them. No, he was sure that, even if there had been such a man, I would not find any books about Conan Doyle in any of the other shops along the Avenue.

I left the shop somewhat confused. I had felt certain of my facts. Now for a dazed moment I began to wonder. After all, I believed just as firmly as the bookseller and the rest of the world in the complete reality of Sherlock Holmes and Watson. I had known them most of my life. I knew better, of course, but the bookseller had seemed so certain and in a sense he was right. Sherlock Holmes and Dr. Watson had lived. They were still alive — like Hamlet and Mr. Pickwick, like Don Quixote, Ivanhoe, Uncle Tom, Peter Pan, Dink Stover, Dr. Kildare, and Perry Mason. They seemed more alive than most of my friends and relatives, the newest astronaut, and the latest Russian politician. I knew them better and liked them better.

Conan Doyle himself must sometimes have been confused as to who made whom and whether he owned Sherlock Holmes or whether Holmes, in one of the unexplained mysteries to which Dr. Watson so often and so tantalizingly refers, had made and owned him. It was as if — in impenetrable disguise — Holmes dogged his footsteps. The great detective seemed always just about to pounce and expose him triumphantly to Inspector Lestrade as the vile perpetrator of some heinous crime; and, as Dr. Watson could testify, the uncanny Sherlock Holmes never failed.

The Strand wanted still more Holmes. It demanded more Holmes. The public would have nothing and no one else. Sherlock Holmes was one of the most celebrated men in all England. He was as familiar as John Bull himself. The public waited with bated breath for news of his next exploit.

Dr. John H. Watson, late assistant surgeon of the Fifth Northumberland Fusiliers, had been invalided out of the British Army and packed back to England on a half-pay pension after taking a Jezail bullet in the shoulder in the Second Afghan War and nearly dying of enteric fever in the base hospital at Peshawur. For a time he stayed at one of the hotels in London's Strand, but his depleted funds made it necessary for him to seek less expensive lodgings. A friend whom he met at the Criterion bar had an idea. That very day he had talked with a young man working in the chemical laboratory at the hospital who was seeking a fellow lodger to share the expense of rooms he had just discovered. They drove around to the hospital to find him, and Dr. Watson met Sherlock Holmes. The next day they inspected the rooms at 221 B, Baker Street — two comfortable bedrooms and a "single large airy sitting-room, cheerfully furnished and illuminated by two broad windows," that was destined to become one of the most famous rooms in the world.

From the first the sturdy, broad-faced Dr. Watson, with his military moustache, his unimaginative honesty, and his utter probity, was fascinated by his strange companion. The lean Sherlock Holmes with his sharp features and penetrating eyes was either busily engaged with his chemical experiments or his untidy notes and scrapbooks or sunk in listless apathy. He was a knife blade of a man with a brain like a computer and muscles like spring wire. When his attention was aroused, he could see through a man or a situation at a glance. When his mind was not actively engaged, he was as lethargic, but not as happy, as a foxhound basking in sunlight.

Though Holmes was an avid student of chemistry, he was not a medical student. He made few references to his past, though Watson discovered later that he had been at Cambridge. Seemingly, he knew everything, and perhaps a little more, about some subjects. He knew nothing, or a little less — for there was no moderation in Holmes — about others.

Of literature, philosophy, and astronomy he knew nothing. He knew little and cared less about politics. He knew something of botany and enough of anatomy. His knowledge of chemistry was profound. His knowledge of sensational literature was immense. He seemed to have at his sharp fingertips all the details of every major crime that had ever been committed, and he learned more every day, for he was a keen student of the daily press.

Their sitting room was always littered with newspapers.

As Watson soon discovered, his fellow lodger's real forte was observation and deduction. He saw everything and with cold, precise logic swiftly deduced from what he saw accurate conclusions that he seemed to reach by clairvoyance but which were completely obvious once he had explained.

Soon Sherlock Holmes divulges his trade. He is a consulting detective, probably the only one in the world. Quickly he demonstrates his abilities by telling Watson why he knew immediately on seeing him that he was an army doctor who had been wounded in Afghanistan. That same morning appears the first of the hundreds of visitors — kings, prime ministers, distraught maidens, harried noblemen, clerks, and tramps — who come to Baker Street to beseech the help of Sherlock Holmes. From their window Watson sees the man across the street checking house numbers against the address on a blue envelope in his hands and wonders who he is.

"You mean that retired sergeant of Marines," says Sherlock Holmes.

Watson is mystified and almost annoyed when Holmes's description proves completely correct.

"How in the world did you deduce that?" I asked.
"Deduce what?" said he, petulantly.
"Why, that he was a retired sergeant of Marines."
"I have no time for trifles," he answered, brusquely; then with a smile, "Excuse my rudeness. You broke the thread of my thoughts; but perhaps it is as well.

So you actually were not able to see that the man was a sergeant of Marines?"

"No, indeed."

"It was easier to know it than to explain why I know it. If you were asked to prove that two and two made four, you might find some difficulty, and yet you are quite sure of the fact. Even across the street I could see a great blue anchor tattooed on the back of the fellow's hand. That smacked of the sea. He had a military carriage, however, and regulation side whiskers. There we have the marine. He was a man with some amount of self-importance and a certain air of command. You must have observed the way in which he held his head and swung his cane. A steady, respectable, middle-aged man, too, on the face of him — all facts which led me to believe that he had been a sergeant."

"Wonderful!" I ejaculated.

"Commonplace," said Holmes, . . .

There you have a scene from *A Study in Scarlet* that was to be repeated scores of times in the Sherlock Holmes stories. Holmes knows at a glance. Watson is mystified. Holmes is contemptuous of anyone too dull to see what is so self-apparent to him. With some condescension but a touch of pride he explains. Watson's admiration knows no bounds, and Holmes almost purrs.

"Elementary, my dear Watson!" is his usual complacent remark.

You should detest the man for his conceit. You don't. You have shared Watson's astonishment and then his belief. Though you consider yourself a little brighter than the good doctor, you are as impressed as Watson — and cleverness is cleverness. You can't deny that, and you have a pleasant feeling that sometimes you can be almost as clever as Holmes himself. Besides, you know that very quickly, very strangely, something exciting is going to happen.

"Quick, Watson! The game's afoot" — and you are off into the fog to outwit a dangerous villain in one of the darkest dens of iniquity in all London.

"Have you your service revolver in your pocket, Watson?" Holmes asks casually. This time you are off from Paddington in a first-class carriage to a remote section of England where strange things have been happening in an ancient manor house set back miles from its neighbors in a dense woods. There will be mystery and suspense, mounting danger, a sweet-faced and innocent girl betrayed or a smooth-faced scoundrel nearly succeeding in his dastardly plans before you and the triumphant Sherlock Holmes and Dr. Watson, puffing a little, are safe home again in the warm sitting room in Baker Street.

If it's, "Quick, Watson, the needle!" you know that the scent is cold. Faced with no entrancing criminal problem, the great detective cannot stand the boredom of everyday existence. He must have recourse to cocaine to endure the almost insupportable dullness of life. He may recover from his drugged stupor in a little while to improvise on his violin, the solacing instrument on which he is almost a virtuoso. Soon he will be raptly analyzing some hitherto almost unknown Oriental poison at his charred and scarred chemistry bench as he smokes cigarette after cigarette or emits clouds of smoke from the curved pipe stuffed with shag tobacco.

He may go without food for days until he emits the triumphant "Ha!" He has found what he is after, something no man has discovered before. This may become the subject of yet another learned monograph by Sherlock Holmes, who has written many papers on many abstruse topics. More than likely, it will be the starting point of a new and even more exciting adventure.

They are all thrillers. Murder, robbery, blackest treason, poisonings, blackguardly deceptions. There is always suspense. Holmes and Watson are often in terrible danger of death in unpleasant forms. The villains are always villains; the heroes are heroes. Black is black and white is white. There are no perplexing subtleties. The heroines are always gentle-voiced, sweet-faced, and pure.

Sherlock Holmes distrusts women. They are too emotional for his cerebral being. Yet he is as chivalrous toward all women as Dr. Watson, and Dr. Watson is as chivalrous as Sir Nigel Loring or Conan Doyle. Women in the Sherlock Holmes stories are ladies upon their Victorian pedestal. When they are in danger, fearful danger, Holmes and Watson come to their rescue with all the gallantry of the medieval knight.

Doyle never lets the reader down in a Sherlock Holmes story. There is always action and plenty of it. The ingenious plot thickens and thickens until suddenly it thins, and virtue, pointed in the right direction by Sherlock Holmes — always to the amazement and profound satisfaction of the worshipful Watson — triumphs.

Usually the story opens with Holmes demonstrating his great powers of deduction on some subject totally unconnected with the story that is about to be told. Almost always, Dr. Watson refers to important and mysterious cases that Holmes has just solved. Conan Doyle could not remember how many times he made offhand reference to imaginary feats performed just before the story in hand begins, cases involving the most highly placed personages in Europe, fabulous jewels, mysterious disappearances, international diplomacy. Often these cases were so secret because of the danger to England or the world that Holmes could not trust even Watson with the facts.

Then there is a knock on the door or there are footsteps on the stairs or a messenger interrupts Dr. Watson in his consulting room, and the new story begins. Because he so sincerely believes it to be true, Dr. Watson always protests that it is the strangest and most exciting that Sherlock Holmes has yet permitted him to tell.

There is something beyond all this that fascinated the readers of *The Strand* and made each story whet their appetite for more. That something, and perhaps it is more important than the plots of the stories themselves, is the warm and living reality of the place, the time, and two remarkable men.

When he was most annoyed with the man he called disparagingly his "most notorious character," Conan Doyle described Sherlock Holmes as a mere calculating machine. He pointed out, too, that Dr. Watson completely lacked a sense of humor and never once told a joke in all the stories. Doyle had concocted Holmes as a device, an infallible device, for deduction, and Watson as a convenient medium through whom he could relate the adventures. Whether Doyle intended it or not — probably because of his skill as an imaginative writer he could not help it — he wrought better than he knew. He made both Holmes and Watson such real and living characters that the public took them to their hearts a long time ago and many years later will not willingly let them go.

Certain elements may be lacking in the characters of the two men, but the lack, together with their marked individualities and eccentricities, only makes them the more human.

Sherlock Holmes is vain, secretive, overbearing, and condescending. He is a dope fiend. His conceit is colossal. He considers himself, most of the time, far and away the most intelligent man he has ever met. He is patronizing to the faithful Watson and often peremptory in his demands. He is scornful of Scotland Yard and of all who pretend even to competency in the field where he acknowledges himself to be the only living expert. So seriously does he take himself that at one point he refuses to consider even a brief absence from England. He says that once the criminal classes learned of his absence there is no knowing what might happen.

Yet Holmes, for all his omniscience, his expertness with the rapier and at Japanese wrestling, his intimacy with most of the greatest personages of several continents, is almost as dependent on Watson's companionship as Watson is on his. Like everyone else, he is often bored, lonely, and restless. He is as helpless as a child who must be continually entertained. When his violin — a Stradivarius worth five hundred guineas which he bought for fifty-five shillings from a Tottenham Court pawnbroker — and his hypodermic of cocaine both fail, he is sometimes driven to lying on his back and punctuating the walls of the Baker Street rooms with revolver shots.

Holmes is capable of intense concentration. On the scent, he cannot be diverted. Obsessed by some captivating, if passing, interest, he cannot let that subject, even the most abstruse, escape until he has plumbed its depths. He writes as an expert on the most widely diverse subjects: tattoo marks, the tracing of footsteps, the distinction between the ashes of the various tobaccos, the influence of trade on the shape of the hand, malingering, the typewriter and its relation to crime, secret writing, the use of dogs in detective work — and then "A Study of the Chaldean Roots in the Ancient Cornish Language," "The Practical Handbook of Bee Culture with Some Observations upon the Segregation of the Queen," and a monograph on the polyphonic motets of Lassus which, according to Watson, experts agreed was the last word on that subject.

Work is all that matters to Sherlock Holmes. A change of work is all the recreation he needs. When he has no work in hand, life loses its savor. He can abide neither it nor himself.

Holmes does not like women. Early he announces to Watson that he will never marry. "Women are never entirely to be trusted," he says in *The Sign of the Four*, " — not the best of them." A few years later he says in *The Valley of Fear*, "I am not a whole-souled admirer of womankind, as you are well aware, Watson. . . .

Should I ever marry, Watson . . ." The coldly rational Sherlock Holmes can be as inconsistent as the next man on this subject, and Watson already knew that his friend was not as unsusceptible to feminine charm as he pretended. There was Irene Adler. After the episode of "A Scandal in Bohemia," Holmes paid her the highest compliment of which he was capable. Ever afterward she was always "*the* woman" to him.

Holmes smokes incessantly, keeping his tobacco in a Persian slipper on the mantelpiece. Though, as Watson comments in *The Hound of the Baskervilles*, he has "a catlike love of personal cleanliness," Holmes is magnificently untidy. He is always hopelessly trying to get his papers in order and working away at huge scrapbooks and his pasted-up encyclopedia of crime. He is as full of tricks as a pet terrier or a spoiled child. He is forever getting himself up in miraculous disguises. You know that this is as much because he craves attention as because the disguise will enable him to catch the evildoer long before the dolts of Scotland Yard even know who the villain is.

When he feels that he has earned it, Sherlock Holmes will pocket a fat fee with frank satisfaction. Yet often he will willingly forgo a fee for the satisfaction of solving a baffling case. He never hogs credit. He is quite resigned to letting Scotland Yard get the public credit for his exploits. It suffices that he, Watson, his impressive clients, and the professionals of detection know that once again he has proved his claim to be considered the world's greatest detective. The game's the thing, and

Holmes plays his game of deduction for the love of it.

Even here, the incomparable Holmes is willing to acknowledge one superior. There is a pleasant touch of honest humility tinged with fraternal devotion in the surprising admission.

Great as Sherlock Holmes is, there is one who is greater. This is his brother, Mycroft Holmes. Mycroft, he admits, possesses the deductive faculty in even greater degree than he. They were descended of country squires, he tells Watson in a moment of confidence, but a grand-uncle was a French artist, and "Art in the blood is liable to take the strangest forms."

Mycroft Holmes, as fat as Sherlock was lean, as sedentary as his brother was active, lodged in Pall Mall. He was in the British government. Sometimes, Holmes confided, he *was* the British government. He held a subordinate position, but this was merely a blind. Others in the government were specialists. Mycroft's specialty was omniscience. He knew everything about everything. The massive Mycroft, seven years Sherlock's senior, seldom left his office or his lodgings. He had no need to. From his armchair he could solve the most difficult problems in crime. Sherlock admitted that again and again he took problems to his brother and received on-the-spot solutions which events proved to be absolutely accurate.

"Elementary, my dear Watson," Holmes might say, dismissing some feat of acute reasoning as a mere bagatelle, an airy nothing, but the reader knows that he is pleased. He often feels warmly toward the unfailing friend he sometimes treats offhandedly but always with affection, even when he teases him about his appearance.

"It's easy to tell that you have been accustomed to wear a uniform, Watson. You'll never pass as a pure-bred civilian as long as you keep the habit of carrying your handkerchief in your sleeve." Dress uniforms are tight-fitting in the British Army. There is usually not a single pocket in tunic or trews.

Holmes can be far more disconcerting than that in analyzing his friend, just for the sport of it.

It was a hot day. Both were feeling languid as they took their ease in 221 b, Baker Street. Watson admits he had fallen into a brown study. Holmes brought him sharply back to reality by casually reading his mind.

Looking absent-mindedly at an unframed portrait of Henry Ward Beecher, whom he admired, had led Watson to an unhappy conclusion about the bitter waste of life in the American Civil War and the uselessness of war as a means of settling international disputes. He had hardly realized what he was thinking about and what had led him to the thought. Holmes knew not only what Watson thought, but also, step by step, how he had arrived at his conclusion. As he well might have been, Watson was aghast and agape with wonder. A few minutes later both were plunged deep into the gruesome "Adventure of the Cardboard Box."

Honest Dr. John H. Watson is endearing always. Stalwart, with a broad, clear face and a cavalry moustache, looking not unlike Conan Doyle, he is all a proper Englishman should be. He is as brave as they come, utterly dependable, dignified, but ready for action at a moment's notice or without. He is unswerving in his loyalty, unquestioning in his devotion to his friend. Watson is a clubman, as a Londoner should be. He has an eye for what he would certainly call "the fair sex," and early on falls prey to the charms of Miss Mary Morstan in *The Sign of the Four*.

He buys a medical practice after his marriage, but he is never out of touch with Holmes, who calls upon him when anything exciting promises. When Holmes does not call, Watson goes round to Baker Street on almost any pretext — or he is accosted on the street by a beggar, a sailor, or an aged and bent old woman who inevitably turns out to be Sherlock Holmes and in need of his help.

When Watson has been alone for a little time after the death of his first wife, Holmes suggests that he sell his small practice in Kensington and rejoin him in the Baker Street rooms. Watson is surprised to sell the practice very quickly at the highest price he dared ask. Only later does he discover — and the fact throws more light on the hidden side of Holmes's nature — that the young doctor who purchased it was a distant relative of Holmes. The great detective had quietly provided the purchase price.

Watson seems to have married a second time. There are indirect references, but that story is never fully told. Characteristically, Watson is too intent on describing Holmes's exploits to detail his own.

Holmes is the marvel of his life. His fascination for Watson never lessens. For him Holmes is as full of surprises after years of intimate companionship as when they first met. There is the day he offhandedly remarks, "Circumstantial evidence is occasionally very convincing, as when you find a trout in the milk, to quote Thoreau's example." Holmes, who reads no books except in connection with his cases, shows that he knows the dry wit of Henry Thoreau in a day when few in England knew his work at all. It must have been the only time the New Englander who lived and wrote so independently impinged on the science of criminal detection.

The golden moments for which Watson waited were different. They were more like those when the two men waited in darkness in the bedroom of the terrible house of Stoke Moran on the western border of Surrey to face the nameless horror that threatened beautiful Helen Stoner. Holmes is speaking.

"Do not go to sleep; your very life may depend upon it. Have your pistol ready in case we should need it. I will sit on the side of the bed, and you in that chair."

I took out my revolver and laid it on the corner of the table.

One moment more precious to Watson than he could say came later in their long association. Both had come very near death in horrible form in "The Adventure of the Devil's Foot." It was Watson, galvanized into action by the sight of Holmes's face, as white and rigid as if he were already dead, who saved them.

"Upon my word, Watson!" said Holmes at last with an unsteady voice, "I owe you both my thanks and an apology. It was an unjustifiable experiment even for one's self and doubly so for a friend. I am really very sorry."

"You know," I answered with some emotion, for I had never seen so much of Holmes's heart before, "that it is my greatest joy and privilege to help you."

It is a perfect friendship. If there is more give on one side and more take on the other, well, friendships are apt to be that way, and this is a friendship between two English gentlemen. Whatever else Holmes and Watson are, they are English gentlemen. Watson conforms more closely to the accepted pattern, but, despite his eccentricities, Holmes is not far off. His oddities are a gentleman's oddities. His class is as unmistakable as Watson's. They are intimates, but they maintain their reserve. They do not pry into each other's personal affairs. They are always "Holmes" and "Watson" to each other, never "Sherlock" and "John." There is none of the cheapening familiarity that might have frayed the friendship of lesser men. They can sit or read silently together in perfect content on those rare occasions when a quiet evening is not interrupted by demands from the outside world for the services of Sherlock Holmes and the trusted companion who has become almost as well known as the great detective himself.

That outside world is the wonderful world of London

in the 1890's. It is a gaslit world, a world of winter snow or steaming summer heat or of pea-soup fog. London was then the largest city on earth. It was the capital of England, the capital of the British Empire, the capital of the civilized world. Holmes and Watson lived in the heart of it, on Baker Street, probably between Blandford and Dorset. The Baker Street station of the Underground was not far away. Portman Place was near by. To the south was busy Oxford Street and Hyde Park; to the north was Marylebone Road. They might adventure into the country — and later in life Holmes lived for a time in Sussex — but both were confirmed city dwellers. Holmes, Watson says in "The Resident Patient," loved to lie in the very center of five millions of people.

When they left their snug lodging, Holmes and Watson either walked into adventure or trotted in a hansom cab, a two-wheeler with the driver perched high above his passengers, or in an open four-wheeler. When Holmes needed sharp-eyed assistants to shadow a suspect or comb some forbidding dockside along the Thames, he had only to call in his Baker Street Irregulars — the cockney gamins of the street.

This was the story that England of 1892 hoped would never end. *The Strand* was determined that it would not as long as A. Conan Doyle could be enticed or bludgeoned into continuing it. Doyle was almost equally determined that it would.

Sherlock Holmes was a nuisance. He was sick of Holmes. Every Holmes story needed a plot as carefully contrived and as detailed as a full-length book. He had to work out every step in advance before he could set Holmes to work from initial problem to final solution, for all detective stories are planned backward.

Doyle felt that he had other and better things to do with his time. He had what he considered far more important writing to do. He made up his mind to cut off the *Strand* editor's pleas by demanding so large a price for any new Sherlock Holmes stories that the magazine could not afford to pay it and its editor would then cease and desist his importunities.

He asked one thousand pounds, about five thousand dollars, for twelve new Sherlock Holmes stories. One thousand pounds, *The Strand* assured him, would be perfectly all right. When might they expect the first story?

Sherlock Holmes had won again. Doyle wrote "Silver Blaze," "The Stock-Broker's Clerk," "The Yellow Face," "The *Gloria Scott*," "The Musgrave Ritual," "The Reigate Puzzle," "The Crooked Man," "The Resident Patient," "The Greek Interpreter," "The Naval Treaty," "The Cardboard Box," — and one more.

The stories appeared one after the other in *The Strand* in London and in *Harper's Weekly* in New York. It was the last of the eleven stories ("The Cardboard Box" was not included) in the volume which became *Memoirs of Sherlock Holmes* that provoked an uproar of disapproval on both sides of the Atlantic. Doyle had made up his mind. If he could do it in no other way, he would do it in this.

On a visit to Switzerland with his wife he had seen

the falls at Reichenbach. It was a fearful place. A torrent fed by melting snow rushed and swirled into an immense chasm formed by high cliffs of wet, black stone, throwing spray high above its churning surface. It seemed the fitting and perfect setting.

Here, in "The Final Problem," Sherlock Holmes met his death at the hands of his relentless enemy, the only foe he deemed worthy of his steel, the infamous mathematician and master criminal, Professor James Moriarty.

5

Too quickly the Doyles' trip to Switzerland was followed by much unhappier events. Mrs. Doyle became unwell. Though she did not seem seriously ill, Conan Doyle quickly sent for a doctor. His diagnosis was grave. Touie was suffering from tuberculosis in the virulent form then known as "galloping consumption." A second doctor confirmed the verdict of the first. They gave Mrs. Doyle only a few months to live.

Conan Doyle was stunned, but he could not and would not accept this death sentence as final, and he threw all his energy into combating the disease. Immediately he abandoned their new London home and took his wife and two small children to Davos, a health resort over five thousand feet high in the Swiss Alps, where his sister Lottie joined the family.

In the high, dry air of Davos amid the beautiful Alpine scenery, Mrs. Doyle's health improved rapidly. The progress of the disease was arrested and soon she was no longer in immediate danger. Thankfully and with his accustomed energy, Doyle threw himself into hard work and hard play.

Davos was a sports center as well as a health resort. Doyle entered into the skating, tobogganing, and bobsledding. There was little else to distract him. He began work on another historical project that had been teasing at his mind. In Switzerland, high in the snow-covered Alps, he started his series of Napoleonic novels and stories: *Uncle Bernac*, *The Exploits of Brigadier Gerard*, *The Adventures of Gerard*, and *The Great Shadow*.

As always, Doyle dug deeply into the history of the period he wished to recreate, versing himself in the details as well as in the broad outlines of the Napoleonic campaigns. Napoleon Bonaparte had ravished Europe from 1796, when he invaded Italy, to his final defeat by the Duke of Wellington at Waterloo in 1815. The Brigadier Gerard series of stories Conan Doyle based largely on *The Memoirs of His Life and Campaigns* by General Jean Baptiste Marbot, Napoleon's dashing leader of light cavalry.

Marbot was a soldier after Doyle's own feudal heart.

To Doyle he was one of the "knightly and gentle souls, playfully gallant, whose actions recall the very spirit of chivalry. A better knight than Marbot never rode in the lists . . ."

Lieutenant Etienne Gerard of Gascony appears for the first time in *Uncle Bernac*, a novel about a young French *émigré* who returns from exile in England to become aide-de-camp to Napoleon; but the swashbuckling, devil-may-care young officer is only a minor character in this Doyle story whose real hero is the emperor himself. Napoleon dominates the story — Napoleon leading his armies, turning strong men faint with a glance, driving Josephine to tears with his brutal speech and actions, checking state accounts like a grubby bookkeeper, approving or disgustedly disapproving the design of dresses for the ladies of his court as if he were the producer of a musical comedy. Doyle shows Napoleon at his best and at his worst. He tosses favors as one tosses bones to a dog. He withholds them just to show he can. He plays at matchmaking like an old maid, yet commands the utter loyalty of resplendent field marshals and ragged privates. Ney, Murat, Bernadotte, Massena, Lannes, Talleyrand live and speak in *Uncle Bernac*, but Napoleon dominates them in the story as he dominated in life.

Etienne Gerard dominates all the other Napoleonic tales. Using a favorite device, Doyle has Brigadier Gerard as an old man look back and enthuse on the glory of his youth and manhood in active service under his beloved emperor. From dashing young lieutenant he progresses through valiant deeds — and imperial favor — to gallant captain, to intrepid colonel, to almost legendary thirty-two-year-old brigadier general commanding the Hussars of Conflans.

These are wonderful tales of battles, duels, secret missions, fiery escapades, and miraculous escapes. Gorgeously uniformed officers and cavalrymen swagger through these stories. Beautiful heroines implore the help of the dashing Gerard, and never in vain. Drums rattle, sabers clash, cannons roar. War horses charge till their stout hearts burst, and brigands burn men alive or, bored with the tameness of that, saw them between heavy boards.

Who is it that slays assassins of a secret order come to Paris to murder Napoleon when Gerard and his emperor hold rendezvous with them in a wood in the dead of night? When all seems lost, on whom does Napoleon call to capture and hide the documents of his reign? Who is it that saves Napoleon after Waterloo? Who, at the very last, conquers the leagues of ocean between them in a go-for-broke attempt to free Napoleon from St. Helena?

The Brigadier Gerard stories are stirring tales of rapier-thrust and pistol fire, and Etienne Gerard is as delightful a character as Conan Doyle ever created.

Gerard's courage is matched only by his boastfulness; his swordplay, by his engaging vanity; his love of his Hussars, by his conviction that he is irresistible to all women. All fire and gallantry in his youth, he is perhaps even more attractive in the years of his nostalgia. His sober self-appreciation is comic and warmly human. You can see him twist the points of his magnificent moustaches to even sharper spikes as he starts to tell "How the Brigadier Slew the Fox."

One day Massena sent for me, and I found him in his tent with a great plan pinned upon the table. He looked at me in silence with that single piercing eye of his, and I felt by his expression that the matter was serious. He was nervous and ill at ease, but my bearing seemed to reassure him. It is good to be in contact with brave men.

"Colonel Etienne Gerard," said he, "I have always heard that you are a very gallant and enterprising officer."

It was not for me to confirm such a report, and yet it would be folly to deny it, so I clinked my spurs together and saluted.

"You are also an excellent rider."

I admitted it.

"And the best swordsman in the six brigades of light cavalry."

Massena was famous for the accuracy of his information.

Conan Doyle considered that "The Man from Archangel," published in *London Society* in 1885 and later reprinted in many collections of his stories, was his finest piece of writing. He may have been right. The story is dramatic and haunting. The reader may well prefer the Brigadier Gerard stories. Fast-moving, brilliantly colored, as amusing as they are exciting, they must certainly be counted among his best.

For the summer of 1894 the Doyles moved from Davos down to Maloja, another health resort in the Engadine valley. Mrs. Doyle's health continued to improve. In the fall they went back to Davos. With his wife comparatively well again and his sister there to help look after her, Conan Doyle felt it safe to accept a pressing invitation.

He had always been attracted by America. American writers had influenced him from the first. He had set some of his earliest stories in the United States. With his young brother Inness, recently graduated from the Royal Military Academy at Woolwich on the Thames below London and now a subaltern (second lieutenant) in the British Army, he sailed for a lecture tour in the United States.

Doyle was delighted with the United States, and those Americans who came to see and hear the big Englishman were delighted with him. He gave his first talk, a sort of trial run, before an audience in a fashionable New York church. He spoke to a very different kind of audience at the popular Daly's Theater in New York one afternoon, at Princeton (which he mistakenly says was one hundred miles away instead of about half that distance) that evening, and in Philadelphia the next day. Under the auspices of a knowledgeable American manager, he visited every town of any size from Boston to Washington and ventured as far west as Chicago and Milwaukee.

The tall, powerfully made Doyle was unaffected in dress or manner. He spoke conversationally from the platform, read informally from popular English authors of the day and from his own work. Mixing the humorous with the serious, he spoke each time for about an hour, tailoring the content of his talk to his audience. When he spoke to the students of Amherst College in western Massachusetts on a cold evening in early November, he told them of his own school life at Hodder and Stonyhurst, then of his years at the University of Edinburgh as a medical student. He told them of his early difficulties as a writer and of the barrier against establishing his name created by the habit of the English magazines of keeping a young author's work anonymous. He described the origin of the Sherlock Holmes stories, read two selections from them, and then read a still unpublished story. The furiously applauding students pled for his early return to Amherst.

Moving a few miles north into Vermont, Doyle stopped for a two-day visit with Rudyard Kipling, who had married an American wife and was living in Brattleboro. The two writers talked shop and amused themselves with hammering golf balls about in a nearby field. Tolerant but puzzled Vermonters watched the antics of the two mad Englishmen, for golf was unknown in that part of New England at that time.

Doyle netted about five thousand dollars from his American tour but took none of it home. In New York, because he believed in it, he invested the whole amount in the new magazine which S. S. McClure was struggling to establish. *McClure's* had already published both "The Final Problem" and "The Slapping Sal" in its first year, 1893. It took Doyle years to realize on his investment, but *McClure's* gradually became a very successful popular magazine and published a dozen more of his stories.

Doyle had enjoyed his busy tour, but it had tired him. He spent most of the return voyage to England in his bunk. He was rested and invigorated when he returned to Davos and his family.

It was now he had one of his most far-reaching sports ideas. Alpine tobogganing, skating, and sledding were not enough for Conan Doyle. He had read of Fridtjof Nansen's exploit in crossing Greenland on skis and wanted to try in Davos what the Norwegian explorer had done. He talked about it with the owner of a sporting goods store in Davos, and they sent to Norway for skis. When they came, they were the first ever seen in Switzerland.

Doyle, the store owner, and his brother strapped on pairs of skis and, after becoming accustomed to them, climbed the Jacobshorn. The ascent was difficult. The descent was thrilling. It intoxicated Doyle to come as close as man can to flying over the surface of the earth. That was the way it seemed to him.

Having accomplished this much, the three men decided on a greater test of their newly learned skill. They determined to cross over a high pass and reach a village in a neighboring valley which in winter was accessible only by a long, roundabout journey. They started out

across fields and slopes, threaded snow chasms and precipices of crusted snow. To negotiate very difficult drops, they fastened their skis together to make impromptu toboggans and coasted down to safety. At one point just as he was about to descend an almost perpendicular declivity, Doyle's skis slipped away from him and he hurtled down on his stomach. They reached their destination to an acclamation of ringing bells and surprised spectators, then made their way safely back. Conan Doyle foresaw correctly — as he foresaw so many things correctly — that some day skiing would be one of Switzerland's most popular winter sports.

Doyle's devotion to sport was lifelong. The iron-muscled big man loved hard, fast games of every kind and believed strongly in their value. He knew that boxing, football, cricket, golf, skiing, riding to hounds, all the outdoors sports he practiced, gave him health and strength. He was convinced that they give any man balance of mind, teach him to give and take blows, to face odds, to accept victory modestly and defeat gracefully.

Despite his beliefs and his assorted skills, he was not as successful in Switzerland at another game which he helped to popularize. Enthusiastically he laid out a golf course about Davos. Just as enthusiastically, or perhaps because they were annoyed or lacked gustatory discrimination, the Swiss cows ate his greens flags as fast as he could put them up.

6

In the fall of 1895, leaving his family again, this time at Caux in France across Lake Geneva from Switzerland. Conan Doyle visited England alone. While he was there an American writer, Grant Allen, better known then than now, gave him an idea. Allen, who had suffered from tuberculosis, told him that he had found the air and climate of Hindhead in Surrey beneficial. Perhaps it would prove as healthful for Mrs. Doyle. Delighted to think they might safely return to England after what seemed, pleasant as it had been, foreign exile in mountain health resorts, Doyle hurried down to Hindhead. Encouraged by what he saw and knew of the place, he bought four acres of land and gave orders for the construction of a large house, really a mansion.

He then returned to Caux and, while the house was being built, started south with his family. They stopped for a few days in Rome, moved on to Brindisi, thence to Egypt, where they spent the winter in a hotel near the Pyramids. Mrs. Doyle liked it and seemed to thrive there. She and his sister Lottie entered pleasurably into the social life about them. Conan Doyle worked away at his Brigadier Gerard stories despite the intense heat, which he disliked. He climbed the Great Pyramid once and decided that was enough of that. He inspected the ruins of an older Egyptian civilization. He took a flyer over the head of a black horse, which then kicked him over the right eye with one of its front hoofs. It took five stitches to close the gash and this left him with a slightly drooping right eyelid. Doyle was thankful his sight was not damaged.

Early in 1896 the Doyles took a tourist steamer up the Nile on a Cook's tour. They explored ancient temples, watched uneasily while bands of dervishes swept down on helpless African villages, talked with British officers on duty in Egypt. With one of these Doyle made a separate journey. Riding in an ornate state coach which had once belonged to Napoleon, they drove across the Libyan desert. At one point they got lost and drove over the hot sands in a great circle. They visited a Coptic monastery near the Natron Lakes and Doyle, a doctor once more, examined the abbot who complained of feeling unwell. Doyle and the colonel were on the way back to Cairo when news reached them that war had been declared between England and the Egyptian Sudan, long a trouble spot in Britain's empire.

Conan Doyle had been writing about the wars of earlier centuries for years. Here was his first chance to see one at first hand. Immediately he cabled the *Westminster Gazette* for permission to act as its honorary war correspondent and got it. He dressed himself in khaki, obtained a huge Italian revolver, bought a canteen and other equipment, and set out by rail for the fighting front. En route he delighted in the British officers — he saw them as larger editions of English public-school boys — who commanded England's Egyptian troops. He marveled at the zeal and industry of the soldiers, and when he reached his destination at Aswan, bought a camel for transport.

He and the camel did not get along. It amazed him that so much black villainy could lurk in such a staid-looking beast, and any arguments between them the camel usually won. Doyle got along better with the correspondents of the other English newspapers who were beginning to arrive at the scene of the war.

With a party of them he reached the outposts of British civilization in that part of Africa at Sarras, fortified now with sandbags and barbed wire. That was the only real sign of war. General Herbert Kitchener, who was to become governor-general of the Sudan and a famous field marshal in World War I, told the correspondents that there could be no battle action against the revolting Sudanese for some time. First he had to collect thousands of camels for his troops. Conan Doyle gladly donated his own unpleasant animal and, with the other correspondents, returned to Cairo.

In April 1896 the Doyles returned to England. In June they moved into their new home at Hindhead, which Doyle named Undershaws.

Conan Doyle had published *Round the Red Lamp* in 1894. As he explained in his preface to this collection of short stories, the red lamp is the usual sign of the general medical practitioner in England. In an advertising blurb the book's American publisher said, "There are no secrets for the surgeon, and, a surgeon himself as well as a novelist, the author has made the most artistic use of the motives and springs of action revealed to him in a field of which he is the master."

The stories themselves are less pretentious than the publisher's confusing praise. Doyle had taken time out from his historical romances to mine his own experience in fifteen tales ranging from the factual to the wildly fanciful. Some of the stories retail incidents which had happened in his career, for they appear as fact in his autobiography; others are as imaginary and as imaginative as he could make them. All of the stories are medical. Some of them are pleasant; more, decidedly, are not.

There is the usual touch of Doyle humor in the story where a young medical student faints in the operating room where he has gone to witness his first surgery. When he regains consciousness, he finds that the operation was never performed. His own imagination had been too much for him. There is intimate knowledge of the medical trade in the story where two young doctors, filled with the latest in medical fads, settle in a district and proceed to take over the practice of an old-fashioned physician who has only the healing touch. Of course, the old doctor has to take care of both young upstarts when they are stricken with influenza.

A young doctor waiting hopefully for custom mistakes the man who comes to read the gas meter for a patient and tries to diagnose his ailments. This was a real incident in young Dr. Doyle's career. So was the story of the gypsy woman and her baby to whom Doyle gave his pennies instead of charging a fee. The most brutal story in the collection is "The Case of Lady Sannox," in which a nobleman husband who is also a skilled actor uses a surgeon to take fiendish revenge on a beautiful but unfaithful wife. "The Los Amigos Fiasco" is even more grisly. Instead of killing a condemned murderer, the electric chair only invigorates him. The executioners then hang the man and shoot him full of holes. He won't die. As Doyle has one of the characters explain, "What you have done with your electricity is that you have increased the man's vitality until he can defy death for centuries." When he let it go, Conan Doyle had a staggering imagination.

A far better book and one which Doyle sometimes thought might prove the most lasting of all his work is *The Stark-Munro Letters*, which appeared in 1895. Smoothly written, packed with fine character drawing, it is a revealing book, not only about Arthur Conan Doyle, but also about any thoughtful young man's approach to life, thought, and his chosen profession.

The letters from "Dr. Stark Munro" to "Herbert Swanborough" go into great detail about Doyle's religious beliefs and his inability to subscribe to the doctrines of any church, including the Catholic, which he abandoned. They talk, with a young man's profundity, of God, women, life, and the discipline of medicine, which the correspondents shared. Even then medicine was not the end-all for Conan Doyle. As he wrote in one letter, ". . . if I can read my own nature, it is not the accumulation of money which is my real aim, but only that I may acquire so much as will relieve my mind of sordid cares and enable me to develop any gifts which I may have, undisturbed." The gift, of course, was his writing.

Doyle added a few incidents and changed names, but the incidents in the letters are for the most part true. He even describes his marriage and the circumstances surrounding it, though, with his penchant for titled gentry and the military, he makes "Winnie La Force," who was really Louise Hawkins, the niece of a retired "General Wainwright" of the Indian Army who had won his Victoria Cross at Lucknow. His Dublin artist uncle becomes "Sir Alexander Munro."

The germ of Doyle's decision to become an eye specialist seems to lie in words he puts into the mouth of "Dr. Cullingworth," who reappears toward the end of the *Letters* to say, "I've taken to the eye, my boy.

There's a fortune in the eye. A man grudges a half-crown to cure his chest or his throat, but he'd spend his last dollar over his eye. There's money in ears, but the eye is a gold mine." Doyle did not find it so.

One incident in the *Letters* was fortunately untrue. A note at the end says that both Dr. Stark Munro and his wife were killed in a railway accident at Christmas 1884. Instead, Conan Doyle and his wife, who was thriving in high, dry, and sandy Hindhead with its shelter from strong winds, were living happily with their children at Undershaws, and Doyle was intensely busy with his sports and his writing. He was a famous writer now, commanding high prices for the products of the pen he drove across the pages of his varied manuscripts.

The Strand in London and *McClure's* in New York abounded with stories by A. Conan Doyle in 1895, 1896, and 1897. Almost every year there was a novel as well as all the stories.

The Strand paid him 1,500 pounds (about $7,500) and his book publishers gave him an advance of another $20,000 or so for *Rodney Stone* in 1896. This was a story of the prize ring into which Doyle poured his own love of boxing and his detailed knowledge of the sport in which he was a formidable amateur.

Doyle's Napoleonic novel *Uncle Bernac* ran as a magazine serial in 1897 in both New York and London and appeared as a book in England the same year. The *Tragedy of Korosko*, in which a party of Nile excursionists of various religious faiths meet a desperate situation, each in his own way, appeared serially in *The Strand* from

May through December of 1897, then was published as a book in both London and Philadelphia in 1898.

The magazines were full of Doyle stories in 1898. In 1899 appeared *A Duet*, a contemporary novel describing the love affair of a suburban man and woman. This was a different kind of story for Doyle, who was usually preoccupied with the past in his romances. That same year Conan Doyle began very much to live in the present himself. The Boer War broke out in 1899, and this time he went to war for real.

This was the imperialistic period of modern European history, with most of the larger European countries vying for colonial possessions and world power. It was the height of England's empire building and empire ruling, but she was having trouble with parts of her global empire, on which it was her proud boast that the sun never set.

About the middle of the seventeenth century Dutch voyagers settled at the Cape of Good Hope on the southern tip of Africa. They built small villages. Their farms supplied the East India Company with food. They pushed north into the wide green country of the African veldt.

In 1814, when the world possessions of the major European powers were reallocated after the defeat of Napoleon, Cape Colony became part of the British Empire. British forces had landed and taken possession in 1806. In 1814 Britain bought the country from the Netherlands. The colony grew and prospered during the nineteenth century. Its population was predominantly Dutch, then British and German. In 1872 it was given complete self-government by Britain, who helped set up the two Boer republics of the Transvaal and the Orange Free State.

In 1893 gold was discovered on the Rand, a rocky ridge at Johannesburg in the Transvaal. The discovery, as in California in 1848, brought a great influx of new settlers, most of them British. To these Uitlanders (Outlanders) the Dutch Boers ("boer" is the English word "boor" in its original sense of "farmer" or "peasant") refused civil rights. These people protested to England, who still held the two self-governing republics as part of her Empire. England was able to do little or nothing. In 1895 a party of the Uitlanders rebelled and, led by Dr. Leander Starr Jameson, raided Johannesburg. The Boers quashed the rebellion harshly. Tensions mounted, and the Boers prepared for war and evidently hoped to provoke it in order to break away completely from Britain. They had almost twice as large a military force as England had scattered over the whole African continent, and far better armament. In 1899 the Transvaal and the Orange Free State declared war on England.

The Boers, on the offensive, acted fast and effectively. They occupied the South African centers of Mafeking and Kimberley. They invaded England's Cape Colony, converged on Natal, and besieged the English forces at Ladysmith. The English, unprepared and on the defensive, did not at first take the war seriously enough. As usual, the British were late in preparation and late to attack. They were defeated at many points with heavy losses.

President Paulus Kruger of the Boers appealed to France and Germany to intervene on the side of the South African republics. Though Germany was tempted to take arms against her hated commercial rival, she did not, but European opinion was aroused against England. England now sent large forces to South Africa, and Lord Roberts, with Kitchener as his chief-of-staff, took command.

In 1900 they relieved and freed the besieged British at Kimberley, Mafeking, and Ladysmith and occupied the Boer capitals of Pretoria and Bloemfontein. The bulk of the Boer forces were defeated and dispersed.

A fighter by nature and a fervent adherent of the British Empire, Conan Doyle, now forty years old, tried to enlist as soon as the war broke out. He was unable to get into the ranks or to obtain a commission when he applied for the Middlesex Yeomanry. Almost immediately he joined the staff of a hospital donated by John L. Langman and, taking his butler, Cleeves, along with him as batman, sailed for Africa as a doctor and general supervisor of the Langman army hospital.

The hospital staff reached Capetown March 21, 1900. They set up their tents outside Bloemfontein April 2. On April 4 the wagonloads of sick and wounded began to lumber in.

The massed Boer forces had been defeated, but the resourceful Boers, skilled riders and expert marksmen, had merely taken to guerilla warfare. Under famed leaders — De Wet, Botha, Oliver, Theron, Delarey, and Jan Smuts, who later became South Africa's leading statesman and a British field marshal in World War II — they raided villages and British posts. They harried troops on the march, destroyed bridges, rails, and communications. One such guerilla force cut off Bloemfontein's water supply, and the hospital had only stagnant well water to fall back upon.

A deadly outbreak of enteric, or typhoid fever, a severe intestinal disorder producing diarrhea, resulted. Sanitation was inadequate. The crowded hospital lacked enough beds and facilities to cope with the epidemic. The sick and dying lay on the ground between the cots of other sick and wounded. The stench was horrible. It was impossible to check the disease and the casualties from it were enormous. Doyle, who says the press dispatches were censored and the news diluted for the public, wrote that the worst surgical ward after a battle would be clean compared to the Langman hospital pavilion. Corpses were wrapped in blankets and tossed into a common grave at the rate of about sixty a day. A vile stench of disease and death rose from the whole city.

Not until a month later when the advancing British forces freed Bloemfontein's water supply did the situation improve. When it was once under control, Doyle and a companion set out for the front. Corpses, dead horses, burned-out farms that had sheltered Boer snipers were part of what they saw. They endured heavy shellfire, saw bearded Boer prisoners, crack Guards regiments, and all the blood and squalor of a full-scale war before duty sent them back to the Langman hospital and their part in it.

Later, Doyle moved up to Pretoria. There he interviewed the commander-in-chief, Lord Roberts, and caught a glimpse of Kitchener, only a glimpse this time of a big man on a huge horse, who waved as he galloped past. After traveling to Johannesburg, where he descended into the Rand mine that had helped cause the trouble, he returned again to his outfit. Conditions there had improved. Things were relatively quiet. He had done what he could. Now he was anxious to get back to England to complete a book about the war and get it into print before his competitors. July 11 he sailed for England. He was in London by early August.

Conan Doyle had begun his history of the South African War before he left England, continued it on shipboard, and written much of it between his medical duties at Bloemfontein. Parts of it were based on conversations with wounded officers and men, on talks with Boers, on interviews with generals. Much of what he wrote was from his firsthand observations. He finished the book at Undershaws and it was quickly published as *The Great Boer War*.

Though Kruger had been forced into exile in 1900, the war was still going on. Kitchener, who had succeeded Lord Roberts as commander, had as many as 200,000 men under his command before it ended. Methodically he was running down, defeating, or capturing the various Boer guerilla leaders. The war was not formally concluded until 1902.

Conan Doyle, the lore of many earlier wars well in

mind, listed in his book's final chapter some of the lessons that could be drawn from the Boer War.

In his opinion, England could forget once and for all her long fear of being invaded. Even without the country's fleet and its professional soldiers, the able-bodied male population, if equipped with modern weapons and thoroughly trained in their use, could repel any enemy who attempted to trespass on the island kingdom.

Doyle advocated less formal drill and more training in marksmanship for the British infantry. The Boers had been sharpshooters. He advised training in taking shelter. The Boers had made use of every swell and dip of the land, every natural fortification, in their guerilla warfare, while British troops had fought in the open. Doyle argued for the use of some form of portable, bullet-proof shield — which is what the tank, developed by the British during World War I, really is.

Doyle found the cavalry most in need of drastic reform. Lances, swords, and revolvers as cavalry weapons, he said, should be placed in museums. Cavalrymen should be trained to fight on foot with rifles after their horses had taken them where they wanted to fight. Doyle had seen that such Boer tactics were effective. So were others.

The Boers had fired their artillery from concealed positions while the British had mounted theirs in straight lines in the open, offering the enemy a perfect target. Greater mobility and greater concealment was what England's artillery needed. He advocated the use of heavier guns and said that he was sure they would be used in future wars. Though many professional soldiers took issue with Conan Doyle's ideas, almost all of them were adopted in World War I. Cavalry proved valueless after the early part of that war. Troops were trained to take cover and fought from concealed trenches. Camouflage was used to hide the giant artillery pieces.

Perhaps Doyle's most foresighted and useful recommendation in *The Great Boer War* was that the regular army should be reduced in strength and used mostly for policing the Empire while a civilian reserve should be enlarged and better trained. Two world wars have now been fought mostly by reserve forces and conscripted armies. Doyle also foresaw correctly that modern armies need more individual intelligence and skills than armies of the past. Recruiters, he said, should pick their men, not just take the nearest. Armies today are composed largely of specialists in many fields.

Patriotism had not gone out of fashion in 1902. It never went out of fashion for Conan Doyle. Though born in Scotland of Irish lineage, he considered himself an Englishman, that is, a Britisher, and England had his whole and unquestioning loyalty. He would fight for it in war, and he would fight for it in peace.

Angered by what he saw as unjust criticism based on ignorance and prejudice, he undertook now, with all the fired energy that was in him, to defend England against her accusers. Throughout Europe, England's detractors during and after the Boer War had pictured her as the bloodthirsty lion descending on the meek and helpless lamb. England was accused of all kinds of assorted atrocities: the murder of civilians, the wanton destruction of property, the use of dum-dum or soft-nosed bullets that inflicted great tearing wounds, the ill-treatment of prisoners. All of these charges, many of them fomented by England's enemies among the Great Powers and given greater circulation by irresponsible journalists who were more interested in putting out a sensational story than an accurate report, Doyle knew to be untrue. He decided to give them the lie throughout the world.

In doing so Conan Doyle made what must be the first use of large-scale propaganda as an instrument of psychological warfare. It was what would now be called a public-relations campaign on an international scale which he undertook and carried to a successful completion. As a result he became an important public figure as well as the famous author he already was.

Working at no profit to himself, using material from *Boer War* and the testimony of responsible witnesses, many of them Boers, in January 1902 he wrote in six days a pamphlet of 140 pages which he titled *The War: Its Cause and Conduct*. It was immediately published and distributed in great numbers throughout England and the United States.

Funds were raised through public subscription, and the pamphlet was translated and published in French, German, Spanish, Portuguese, Hungarian, Norwegian, and Welsh.

Point by point *The War* refuted all the charges which had been made against England. It disproved all the accusations which had been made against the British troops, showed that farms had been burned only because they harbored armed enemies attacking the British forces, and defended the use of concentration camps in which Boer civilians had been placed for their own safety and in which they had been well cared for. It traced the charge of using dum-dum bullets to its source and showed that the British had used none in the conflict.

Doyle's treatment of his subject was reasonable, clear, and informed throughout. The utter honesty of the writer was unmistakable. His work was effective and did much to right Great Britain in world opinion. It did more.

In his preface Doyle wrote that, either through ignorance or apathy, the British had always been slow to state their case to the world. In *The War* he showed England the value and importance of well-executed propaganda, an instrument which England was quick to use in World War I and later. Propaganda is now an accepted weapon in war and in the armed truce between nations which is now called peace. Doyle was pleased and perhaps quietly agreed when Herbert Gwynne, a war correspondent he had first known in the Egyptian Sudan who had become editor of the London *Morning Post*, wrote him that he considered his work during the South African War equal to that of a successful general.

The British government and its new king certainly thought well of what Doyle had accomplished for his country. In 1902 he was offered a knighthood. It seems odd that this man who was descended from titled figures and who had been bred in the traditions of knighthood was determined not to accept it. He felt that the title had become merely the badge of the successful and not always too ethical businessman and of the ambitious politician. It was Mary Foley Doyle who insisted sharply that he accept. Chiding him as if he were still a boy who had not learned his lessons in chivalry as thoroughly as she was determined he would, his mother pointed out that it would be an insult to his king, Edward VII, were he to reject the proffered accolade.

For his patriotic services to England, Doyle emerged from Buckingham Palace on Coronation Day, August 9, 1902, as Sir Arthur Conan Doyle, Deputy Lieutenant of Surrey.

An old enemy caught up with him now. He had skulked for two years in Tibet, then, assuming the Norwegian alias of Sigerson, conducted some rather remarkable explorations into unnamed lands. He had spent some time after that in Persia, some in Mecca, some in Khartoum, then returned to France before daring to venture back into London. There were those who thought he had died, but they knew also that resurrection was not impossible for a man of his unique powers.

It was Sherlock Holmes.

7

Dartmoor in Devon in the southwest corner of the British Isles is a windswept, rain-driven waste of upland pasture about twenty-five miles long by twenty miles wide. It is one of the bleakest and wildest tracts in all England. There are few trees. The bare, rolling land is covered with gorse and heather, with outcroppings of granite among the treacherous peat bogs. Wild ponies run free over the barren hills. The air is wet-cold. It is a lonely, desolate region, with scattered sheep farms the only habitations except Bronze Age huts and other stone relics of prehistoric man.

The center of the trackless moor — for there are few roads — is dominated by the grim prison at Princetown. Days are dark on Dartmoor, and nights are black with only here and there a distant light glimmering through the mists. A comfortless wind is the only sound.

Conan Doyle had never seen Dartmoor when in the spring of 1901 he went on a golfing holiday with a friend, Fletcher Robinson. One Sunday afternoon when it was too cold and windy to play they sat before a fire in their room in a Norfolk village inn, and Robinson told him some of the legends of the moor. Doyle was fascinated by the mysteriousness and eeriness of Dartmoor as the other described it.

The plot of a new thriller already forming in his mind, Doyle went with Robinson on a visit to Dartmoor a few weeks later. They stayed in Princetown. The stark prison, which housed England's worst prisoners, is visible from everywhere in the small town. It stands apart on ground as bleak as its cold outlines. Doyle had already used it in his Brigadier Gerard stories, for it held French prisoners during the Napoleonic wars, just as it held American prisoners during the War of 1812.

The two men walked for miles over the bleak moors. They saw the frightening bogs, explored the stone huts. The dark and dismal atmosphere of Dartmoor gripped Doyle. He had to get it on paper. Story and characters took shape. Plot and setting were perfect for a Sherlock Holmes story, but he had killed Holmes. Doyle solved this problem by having Dr. Watson tell the story of *The Hound of the Baskervilles*, dedicated to Fletcher Robinson, as an earlier Holmes adventure that he had not told before.

Every reader of Conan Doyle knows that tense and eerie tale, one of Doyle's finest, almost frightening in its creepiness, which involves Holmes and Watson, Dr. Mortimer, Sir Henry Baskerville, Selden, the Stapletons, the huge, infernal hound luminous in the black Dartmoor night, and murder most vile. For sheer transfer of all the threatening ghostliness and the engulfing horror of place and circumstance, Doyle never bettered his Dartmoor thriller about the Great Grimpen Mire and the spectral hound.

The Hound of the Baskervilles, Sidney Paget again the illustrator, ran in *The Strand* from August 1901 through April 1902. McClure, Phillips published it as a book in New York at the same time that George Newnes published it in London. Holmes, though still presumed dead, was back. In reality, he had never left. People read and reread the Sherlock Holmes stories, and they watched him in flesh and blood on the stage. The American actor William Gillette had been acting the part on the stage since 1899 in hundreds of appearances in many places, and was to go on acting in the play he had arranged from many of the Holmes stories until a few years before his death in 1937. America knew Sherlock Holmes almost better than England knew him. The clamor in both countries was for more Sherlock Holmes, always more Sherlock Holmes. Yet Conan Doyle had tossed Holmes to certain death over the cliff at Reichenbach in 1893.

Ten years later, in 1903, an American magazine publisher offered Doyle five thousand dollars each for six new stories about Sherlock Holmes. And they would pay the same amount for each of as many more as he would write. These were real dollars, tax-free in the United States, whose purchasing power was three or four times more then than now. *The Strand* would at the same time pay more than half that amount for British magazine rights to each new short story about Sherlock Holmes. Doyle would get additional sums from the sale of the English and American book rights.

Impatient as he was with Sherlock Holmes, famous as he was and as well situated financially as all his successful short stories and novels had made him, Conan Doyle could not turn down such an offer.

He brought Sherlock Holmes back to life. For the first and last time in his adventurous career, Dr. Watson fainted. Holmes, of course, had never been killed. Through his knowledge of Japanese wrestling, Sherlock Holmes had broken the grip of his executioner. It was not he but Professor Moriarty who had been dashed to his death at Reichenbach. Only his brother Mycroft had known that Sherlock Holmes was still alive. Holmes had not dared let Watson know for fear he, too, be in danger from Colonel Moran and others of Professor Moriarty's gang who still pursued him, for they knew he was still alive.

Mycroft had kept his brother's Baker Street lodgings and all his papers intact during his three years of absence on the Continent and in the Orient. In no time at all, Watson, his revolver in his pocket, is seated beside Sherlock Holmes in a hansom, and they are off into the hair-raising "Adventure of the Empty House."

Conan Doyle's hand had not lost its cunning in the ten years of his freedom from the keen-eyed surveillance of the relentless Sherlock Holmes. If anything, his skill, sharpened by all the other books and stories he had written in that packed decade of his life, had increased. The new Holmes stories were as firm, as convincing, and as gripping as the first.

Rapidly Conan Doyle wrote the thirteen stories that make up *The Return of Sherlock Holmes*. It was in *Collier's*, long a popular weekly magazine in the United States until it ceased publication in 1956, that the first of them appeared in 1903: "The Empty House," "The Norwood Builder," "The Dancing Men." They were followed by ten more, beginning with "The Solitary Cyclist," in 1904. At the same time, of course, the stories were appearing in *The Strand*.

Rave reviews greeted *The Return* when the book was published. John Dickson Carr describes vividly the scene in London when Sherlock Holmes reappeared. The railway bookstalls in London were mobbed. It was worse, one woman reported, than anything she had ever seen at a bargain sale. Queues of eager purchasers formed in Southampton Street to grasp for copies, just like the lines at a theater or movie house for a smash hit. The publishers could not print copies fast enough. Sherlock Holmes was home again in Baker Street. Dr. Watson was with him. London was complete again. The world was safe again, and life, gone dull while Holmes lay at the bottom of the Reichenbach Falls (actually he was visiting the head lama at Lhasa and later the Khalifa at Khartoum, then working on coal-tar derivatives in a laboratory at Montpellier) was alive again.

Protest as he might, Conan Doyle would have been a strange man indeed if he were not pleased. He was pleased — with reservations. Already he was busy with other projects, sporting, literary, and even political. Once more he intended to write the kind of novel he preferred to write and which he considered far superior to stories about Sherlock Holmes, pamphlets about war, plays, or any of the other outpourings of his versatile talent. The very success of *The Return* was a goad. This lionizing of Sherlock Holmes was delaying once more full appreciation of what he insisted was his more serious and more important writing.

In spacious Undershaws at Hindhead in 1904 he began to study the Middle Ages again, taking exhaustive notes for a new historical romance of the time of King Edward III. For his hero he chose Sir Nigel Loring, the undersized, middle-aged knight he had celebrated in *The White Company*. This time he set the story twenty years earlier so that he could present Nigel in the full glory of his youth. Conan Doyle had written the new Sherlock Holmes stories for money. He wrote *Sir Nigel* for love.

Lacroix's *Middle Ages*, Oman's *Art of War*, Hewitt's *Ancient Armour*, Froissart's *Chronicles*, Hargrove's *Archery*, and a score of comparable books still lay on his study table as he wrote the introduction to *Sir Nigel*. He had practically memorized them. If he had been unable to combine and transfer their effect, the fault was his, he said. He did combine and transfer, but he did more. The facts may have come out of these books, but the spirit of *Sir Nigel* came out of the inner Arthur Conan Doyle. He was back now where he really lived, amid the silken banners and the shining swords and lances of chivalry.

"The fantastic graces of chivalry lay upon the surface of life, but beneath it was the half-savage population, fierce and animal, with little ruth or mercy. It was a raw, rude England, full of elemental passions and redeemed only by elemental virtues. Such I have tried to draw it." So Doyle wrote, but it was the graces he emphasized. The sports of the chase and of the lists, the chivalric gallantry of Sir Nigel and his fellows, men of gentle birth and coat armor seeking honor and glory through the prowess of their arms, loyalty to king, country, and the code of the golden spur; it was these Conan Doyle loved and applauded.

The story opens in the spring of 1348 after the winter of the Black Plague. Barons and villeins, monks and franklins, knights and wights had died, for the disease that sent them raving with gross boils and hideous blotches on their skin had been no respecter of persons. Whole villages had been virtually wiped out. The dead had rotted by the roadside for want of the quick to bury them. "Then at last the spring came, with sunshine and health and lightness and laughter — the greenest, sweetest, tenderest spring that England had ever known."

It was spring, too, for Sir Nigel, twenty-two, the blood of generations of soldiers thrilling in his veins, debonair, an expert horseman, a master of all field sports. He lived with his grandmother, Dame Ermyntrude, on the small estate which was all the rapacious Cistercian monks had left them of the vast landholdings of the Lorings. As Conan Doyle's mother had trained him in his boyhood at Edinburgh, Dame Ermyntrude trained her grandson in heraldry and inculcated in him all the knightly ideals of his forebears. Like Conan Doyle, Sir Nigel responded with all his body, mind, and heart.

The slight, lionhearted youth had just ridden and tamed a fierce yellow war horse which had trampled several of the monks. Because no one else could rule him, the abbot gave Nigel the horse. Then the abbot's summoner sent king's agents and archers to enforce new demands on the Lorings, claims dating back to before the death of Nigel's father. When Nigel had them thrown into a swamp he was hauled before the abbot and sentenced to six weeks on bread and water. He is in the act of defying abbot, abbey, and all, when Sir John Chandos, "the flower of English chivalry," appears with the news that King Edward is en route to spend the night at the Lorings' manor house of Tilford.

The adventure never slows from that point. Jousts follow falconry and the hunt. Valiant deeds cap one another. Sir Nigel goes as squire to Sir John Chandos in the train of King Edward. Before he leaves to fight for England in France, he swears to Lady Mary Butteshorn before the shrine of St. Catherine that he will send back tokens of three great deeds done in her honor, then return to claim her hand.

This is historical romance in the grand manner, done with the skill, grace, and enthusiasm Doyle brought to his tales of knighthood and informed by his own knightly code. It is adventure that thrills with its intensity and throbs with its author's convictions. Doyle was in love with this novel, and when he had finished it, believed he had written his finest book. "The Man from Archangel" might be his finest piece of writing and *The Stark-Munro Letters* his most enduring book, but this was his great and shining romance. In it he felt that he had reached the very peak of his performance as a writer. By it he would stand or fall. *Sir Nigel* together with *The White Company* was, in his opinion, his master work. He was elated as he started for Edinburgh in pursuit of still another objective.

Most writers are writers merely. They are thoughtful, perhaps talented, reflective, sedentary men. Doyle was thoughtful, talented, reflective, and everything else that a writer must be, but he was first a man of action. He was never content to be merely spectator and recorder. He had to be a driving participant whether in the practice of medicine, boxing, cricket, football, war — he saw them all as manly activity, and war as the knights saw it, perhaps the most thrilling and ultimate sport. He was a competitor. He had taken an important part in national life after the Boer War. He had gone into politics as early as 1901.

He had stood for Parliament for Central Edinburgh that year. His immense popularity and his effectiveness as a speaker had almost guaranteed the home-town boy the election when he was attacked by "an evangelical fanatic" — the phrase is Doyle's — for his Roman Catholic upbringing. He lost the election.

In 1905 Doyle tried again, this time for the Parliamentary seat of Hawick, Galashiels, and Selkirk in Scotland. He put all his effort into this campaign, expending all his time and considerable money in an all-out attempt to win. He endured heckling from the speaker's platform but held his own in rough and ready repartee. Rowdies seeking amusement at the expense of any candidate tried to break up his meetings. Doyle ignored or stilled them. He suffered all the indignities that accompany the soliciting of votes for office anywhere.

Doyle particularly resented the brazen, back-slapping familiarity of complete strangers. A man of reserved and even courtly manner, he took such liberties with no man. When a supporter greeted him boisterously on a railway platform and shook his hand so hard that his signet ring cut into his finger, Conan Doyle exploded in wrath. That was too much. That was much too much. He blew up the offender with a blast of whaler profanity that surprised him almost as much as it shocked his supporters, and left. He lost the election.

The next year Conan Doyle suffered a far worse defeat. Through unceasing care and atention he had managed to forestall the inevitable conclusion for thirteen years beyond what the doctors had set as a terminal date.

It could be put off no longer. In 1906 Louise Hawkins Doyle died. She had been his life's companion from his days as a struggling young doctor in Southsea into the years of his success as a writer and a public figure. Her death depressed Conan Doyle deeply, and the depression lasted. For a time he could settle to nothing. When a diversion offered he seized on it gladly.

Sir Arthur Conan Doyle was Sherlock Holmes. The public insisted on this and would not be turned from its belief. Often the confusion of identities infuriated him. He was Sherlock Holmes, of course, as any writer is all of his character creations, but the coldly deductive detective represented only a small part of his full and many-faceted nature. When pressed, he had to admit that he was Holmes. In fact, according to Adrian M. Conan Doyle, his father told an American journalist in 1918 that if anyone was the actual Sherlock Holmes, he had to confess that he was. He was Sherlock Holmes and the public believed that anything which Holmes could do, Sir Arthur Conan Doyle could and would do.

Through Holmes, Doyle's influence on actual criminology was far-reaching. His methods were adopted and used in the training of detective forces in many places. Scotland Yard put some of Holmes's practices to use. The French Sureté named its Lyons crime laboratories in Doyle's honor. The police college of China paid him the tribute of acknowledged imitation. When Doyle was called upon to emulate the deeds of Sherlock Holmes, he not only could but he did.

Characteristically, it was not to demonstrate his prowess but to right a wrong that Conan Doyle called his detective powers into play. Undue familiarity angered him; injustice enraged.

The Church of England's vicar in a Staffordshire village was a Parsee, an Indian, who had married an English wife. They had a son and a daughter. The son, who had been a brilliant law student, practiced as a solicitor in Birmingham. In 1903 the vicar's family was plagued by a series of anonymous letters, threatening and obscene, and made the victim of unpleasant practical jokes. Other people received letters of the same kind.

At about the same time an epidemic of horse- and cattle-maiming broke out. Under cover of darkness someone slashed cows and ponies in the most cruel and sickening fashion and left the animals to bleed slowly to death. The anonymous letters accused George Edalji, the dark-skinned son of the Indian father and English mother.

For a long time the police were unable to uncover the culprit or culprits. Finally they seized on the accused Edalji as the criminal who was both writing the letters and sadistically torturing the animals. On no evidence at all, almost in spite of the evidence, he was tried and convicted. He was sentenced to seven years of penal servitude. The young man was dark, of different racial extraction, and so shortsighted as to be nearly blind. To the ignorant and prejudiced of the village this was evidence enough that he had perpetrated the crimes.

While Edalji was in prison both the anonymous letters and the maiming and killing of the helpless animals continued. It was obvious he had committed neither crime.

In 1906 he was released from prison without pardon or exoneration. He was a convict who had to report regularly to the very police who had concocted the evidence against him. He had been disbarred as a lawyer, and thus could not earn a living through the practice of his profession. His appeals to official sources were ignored. In desperation George Edalji wrote to Conan Doyle, enclosing newspaper clippings of the crimes, his arrest, trial, and imprisonment, and sought his help in having his name cleared and his full civil rights restored.

Doyle was convinced that Edalji had told the simple truth. The evidence against him had been both inadequate and contrived. His trial had been a farce and his punishment completely undeserved. Angrily, Conan Doyle set out to obtain justice for a wronged man.

He studied the trial records and all the other evidence in the case, traveled to Staffordshire and interviewed the family, examined the scenes of the crimes. He arranged to meet George Edalji and with his oculist's eye saw immediately that the dark-visaged young man suffered so severely from astigmatic myopia (shortsightedness and distorted vision) that he was partially blind in daylight and almost totally blind at night. He could not possibly have approached the animals and committed the mutilations for which he had been condemned.

After spending months investigating, Doyle wrote an exposé of the whole case in a series of articles, "The Case of Mr. George Edalji," which began January 11, 1907, in the London *Daily Telegraph*. Other newspapers picked up the stories. Various publications, men, and organizations spoke out with Conan Doyle on behalf of the wronged man. Doyle aroused all England to indignant protest at the unjust treatment Edalji had suffered.

The English government was forced to make some show of acknowledgment. A committee was appointed. It determined that George Edalji had been wrongly found guilty of the animal maiming and censured those who had convicted him. The committee held, however, that he might have written the anonymous letters accusing himself. It claimed that Edalji had thus helped bring on his own plight and was therefore entitled to no compensation for his three years of unjust imprisonment. Though the Law Society immediately readmitted George Edalji to practice, he still stood condemned for an act he had not done.

The illiterate but cunning anonymous letters were still being written and sent. Doyle himself received seven of them threatening his life. He boiled into action again and wrote another series of articles, "Who Wrote the Letters?" His opinion of government bureaucracy had never been higher than bureaucracy in England or elsewhere generally deserves. He found now that the trade-union solidarity of government workers, from the highest to the lowest ranks, is impregnable. It is a mutual protective society. None will admit error or misconduct on their own part or on the part of any other member.

Even when he plunged further into his investigations and discovered the actual criminal, a sailor on a cattle ship who had been a butcher's apprentice with a record of writing anonymous letters, the government would neither accept nor act upon the conclusive evidence. Officialdom would not exonerate George Edalji. Yet Conan Doyle in the character of Sherlock Holmes had cleared him in the eyes of the public.

Conan Doyle was to appear a number of times as Sherlock Holmes when people in distress appealed to him. In December 1908 an elderly woman living alone in an apartment in Glasgow was robbed and brutally murdered. A German Jew with an unsavory reputation and a bad record was arrested for the crime on wildly circumstantial evidence as he stepped off the *Lusitania* in New York shortly afterward. Though he screamed protestations of innocence — of utter ignorance of the very existence of the victim — Oscar Slater was hauled back to Scotland, tried, convicted, and sentenced to death. Just the day before he was to be hanged the death sentence was commuted to life imprisonment.

Once more an appeal was made to Conan Doyle. Once more examination of the evidence convinced him that an innocent, if generally unpleasant, man had been victimized by unreliable witnesses, police persecution, and questionable legal proceedings. Doyle attacked the decision in the press, fomented inquiry into the conduct of the whole matter. In a booklet, "The Case of Oscar Slater," he exposed the fallacies in the evidence and in the defense of the condemned man. A police officer who agreed with Doyle and a defense lawyer were persecuted for the stand they took against the verdict. Conan Doyle could not budge the authorities, and Oscar Slater remained in prison for eighteen years for a crime he had known nothing about.

Conan Doyle, who had never ceased to agitate for Slater's release, then forced a retrial of the case in Edinburgh. This time Slater was found wholly innocent and was awarded compensatory damages of about $30,000. Oscar Slater was vindicated and so was Sir Arthur Conan Doyle as his champion.

Doyle, in these years, struck out at cruelty and injustice wherever he found it. He championed far-reaching military reforms, reform of England's antiquated divorce laws. He waged war against the cruel mistreatment of the African natives in the Belgian Congo. The creator of Sherlock Holmes — but also of crusading knights and honest fighting men like Sir Nigel, Brigadier Gerard, Samkin Aylward, Sir Gervas Jerome, and Micah Clarke — was a power in forming public opinion and, when he was convinced that there was a wrong to be righted, no man to trifle with.

In a quiet ceremony in London, September 18, 1907, Sir Arthur Conan Doyle married Jean Leckie, a young and beautiful woman whom he had known well for over a decade and who was a close friend of his mother and sister. An expert horsewoman who had studied voice in Germany and Italy, the new Lady Doyle was the youngest daughter of an old Scottish family living in Sussex. So that his wife might be near her family, Doyle, after ten years at Hindhead in Surrey, bought and enlarged a home near Crowborough in Sussex and named it Windlesham. Here, except when they were on their frequent world travels and Doyle was in service in World War I, with Lady Doyle, his son and daughter by his first marriage, and three more children born of his second, Doyle spent the remainder of his colorful and busy life.

The years just before World War I were pleasant and happy years in England, and they were pleasant and happy years for Conan Doyle. There was an enormous billiard room in big, five-gabled Windlesham. Often it was filled with guests as celebrated as their host: writers, generals, cabinet members, actors, detectives, sporting figures. The Doyles were frequently up in London where Doyle was producing plays he had adapted from his Holmes and Brigadier Gerard stories and from his novel of the prize ring, *Rodney Stone*. The plays were well attended by applauding audiences but, like most theatrical producers, Doyle had his financial ups and downs. At one point when he had leased a London theater for six months he might have lost heavily had he not packed it with *The Speckled Band*, a play based on one of the original *Adventures of Sherlock Holmes*.

Twice the Doyles made extended Mediterranean voyages, visiting Greece, Egypt, and the Dardanelles. In Constantinople, the Sultan of Turkey bestowed the Order of the Medjidie on Sir Arthur Conan Doyle and the Order of the Chavakat on Lady Doyle. Secretly they were admitted to the Mosque of Sophia during the Night of Power and looked down on twelve thousand worshipers at their devotions under the spell of priests screaming from their high pulpits.

Drawn by his sporting instincts, Conan Doyle covered the marathon in the Olympic games of 1908 for London's *Daily Mail.* He was thrilled by the spectacle and the gallant race run by an Italian, Dorando. At home he had his cars, even a motorcycle, his golf, his billiards. His novel about the prize ring and its stage presentation had made his name so well known in boxing circles that the editor of the *New York Daily Telegraph*, seconded by the promoter Tex Rickard, tried to get him to referee the world championship heavyweight title bout between Jim Jeffries and Jack Johnson at Reno, Nevada, in 1909. This would have added another headliner to the bill, a box-office attraction almost equal to "the fight of the century" itself. Doyle was tempted and very nearly accepted, but he had too many other games in hand, too much writing to do, too many moral obligations.

He appealed to President Theodore Roosevelt, whom he admired as an apostle of the strenuous life and himself a sportsman, to use his enormous influence in attacking the rule of the Belgian Congo under King Leopold. In 1909 he published his *Crime of the Congo,* describing the torment and torture of the natives and calling for reform. He came out in favor of home rule for Ireland. He took on both England's church and state in his all-out fight for reform of the divorce laws.

The massive Conan Doyle thundering out his strong opinions in the billiard room at Windlesham or broadcasting them in the press and in books, the world-famous "Sherlock Holmes" who had successfully applied his detective swill to cases in real life, the titled sportsman respected in professional and amateur circles alike, was a power in the land. Sometimes he must have marveled at what had happened to him — or what he had made to happen.

The contrast between his present affluence and the penury of his early days in Southsea, when he cooked over an amended gas jet and polished his brass plate surreptitiously at night, and Inness in page's dress rushed to answer the door for the occasional welcome patient, must often have occurred to him. The contrast between Sir Arthur Conan Doyle fighting for reforms in England, Ireland, and Africa and the schoolboy that he had been, battling his enemies on the Edinburgh streets, must have occurred to him too.

Doyle played cricket so well that he played for his county against other English counties. He played for the Marylebone Cricket Club itself at its internationally known Lord's Cricket Ground. He was so expert at billiards that a professional he beat twice with casual ease mistook him for the professional billiards champion of the day.

More important, he was so well-established and popular a writer that he could virtually name his own price for his work. His stories were appearing steadily in *The Strand* in England and in *Collier's, Scribner's,* and *The American Magazine* in the United States. In 1911 he published the amazing total of seven books in one year, and he was busy with writing far different from any he had done before.

Working with glee and gusto Conan Doyle invented

a new character. This was the great, the magnificent, the unique, the marvelous — just a few of the adjectives which he seriously and proudly applied to himself — Professor George Edward Challenger.

Black-bearded, with huge shoulders and long, swinging arms, Professor Challenger, by his own admission, was the world's greatest zoologist. He admitted no one worthy to compete with him for that distinguished title. Hairy-chested and built like an ape, he was also violent-tempered, pugnacious, and quite capable of demolishing any opponent in the fisticuffs it delighted him to engage in.

Doyle delighted in Professor Challenger. In the evening, after he had been writing about him all day, he read parts of the Challenger stories aloud to his wife and any guests who were present, laughing, gesturing, living the part as he read. He even got himself up in Challenger costume, complete with long black beard, too small straw hat, and a heavy German accent. Doyle was vastly amused by this; some of his friends were dismayed.

Challenger hated the telephone company. He hated newspapermen. He hated the scientific colleagues who scoffed at his wildly fantastic and vividly reported discoveries. He threw people out of his house, condemned everyone and everything in sight, stormed at his fellows, and had a roaring good time for himself, Conan Doyle, and every reader of *The Lost World*.

The story is told by Edward D. Malone, athletic young reporter for a London newspaper. It opens at a great meeting of scientists in London, which turns into a

131 |

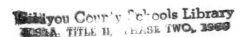

riot as almost all of them deride Professor Challenger's reports of a lost world in South America where apemen, dinosaurs, and various other scarifying prehistoric animals and reptiles live just as they had lived millions of years before. Challenger defies the entire meeting and offers to lead an expedition to the lost world to prove his contentions. One of the most doubting of the doubters, Professor Summerlee, whose specialty is comparative anatomy; Lord John Roxton, world traveler and big-game hunter; Challenger; and Edward Malone set out.

Conan Doyle, who usually kept his imagination well under control, loosed it uncontrolled in the science-fiction story which follows. It is as exciting as battle, murder, and sudden death, as terrifying as the mammoth reptiles and enormous snakes in the dark, steaming jungle, as humorous as the blustering Challenger and the brittle Summerlee can make it. The four men do battle with huge and repulsive creatures. They are captured by apemen who would hurl the three lesser men off a high cliff onto nicely pointed stakes below but make a king of Professor Challenger, whom they recognize as one of themselves. Miraculously, the party escapes and joins forces with a tribe of Indians to fight and defeat the apemen.

Triumphantly the quartet returns to London with irrefutable proof of the existence of the lost world. They even take with them a creature shaped and visaged like the devil himself. It escapes from the platform in packed Queen's Hall and flies on leathery ten-foot wings through a window into the London night.

The scoffers are now all entranced believers. Shouting and cheering, they hoist Challenger, Summerlee, Roxton, and Malone to their shoulders and bear them down Regent Street in a great triumphal procession.

The Lost World is a dazzling book. It is a rollicking book. It is even, somehow, a convincing book. As usual, Doyle had worked up his background thoroughly. Scientists were impressed by his accuracy in detail. Many of the gullible read the fantasy as fact. If he read it, Sherlock Holmes probably suspected the literal truth of parts of the tale, but Dr. Watson was probably as excited and as convinced as everyone else. *The Lost World* ran as a serial in *The Strand* in 1912.

The next year Professor Challenger outdid even his exploits in South America. He prevented the end of the world, at least for himself and his friends. As, from the news of unexplained illness and death on far distant continents and in widely separated places, he had suspected it might, the world swims into a belt of poison ether. Summerlee, Roxton, Malone, and he survive what seems the world's final night by following his instructions. The next day (in Challenger's 20-horsepower Humber) they drive into London. The entire city lies in apparent death. There is no sound or movement. People lie or stand rigid in the streets, in buses, halted in the act of whatever they were doing. Police on traffic duty have frozen where they stood.

Fortunately, it is not all exactly what it seems. There is a happy ending to Doyle's stark tale of *The Poison Belt*.

In a shorter science-fiction piece, *The Disintegration Machine*, Doyle seemed to foretell the smashing of the atom. Certainly he pointed out vividly the force of such a weapon in warfare. This was in 1929. Before this he had involved Professor Challenger in still other mysteries in *The Land of Mist*.

Doyle was an early automobile enthusiast. He thought of driving as another sport, and he went at it hard. Once when one of his cars overturned he was pinned beneath it. Enormously strong as he was, he kept the car from crushing him by holding up the ton weight on his spine just below the neck until he was freed. It was a feat, he said, which he had no desire to repeat.

In 1911 he accomplished a pleasanter, though not entirely pleasant, motoring feat. Prince Henry of Prussia, commander of the German Navy, organized an international road competition between teams of German and English drivers. Each owner had to drive his own car and carry as observer an army or navy officer of the other country. Some fifty German cars, mostly Mercedes and Benz, were entered, and some forty English. Lady Doyle rode with her husband in the run that started in Hamburg, ran north through Germany, sailed for Southampton, then went north to Edinburgh and back down through England to London.

The British won the run, which was a test of skill and endurance rather than speed. This was a satisfaction to the competitive Conan Doyle, but the behavior of the German drivers and observers was not. He disliked most of the German officers on the run, deplored their conduct, and distrusted their intent, Doyle was convinced now that a European war would soon break out and knew that Germany would be the enemy. Others shared his realization, which was sharpened by his experience in driving his 16-horsepower Dietrich-Lorraine landaulette through Germany and England.

With his quick intelligence and ready imagination, Doyle envisioned what kind of war it might well be and early foresaw what would be one of the greatest threats to England. He put his ideas in order and wrote an article which was published in the *Fortnightly Review* in mid-1913, a year before the outbreak of World War I.

In "England and the Next War" Doyle talked of other things, but what he emphasized was the danger England faced if submarines were used against her. Swarms of enemy submarines in the English Channel and the Irish Sea could cut off England's food supply, and five-sixths of England's food came from abroad. He prophesied that ships of other nations as well as England's would be torpedoed without warning by submarines.

Doyle treated the same subject in story form in *Danger*, which was published in *The Strand*, then later as a book. In this story one of the smallest of the European powers loosed a flotilla of eight submarines against merchant ships and liners bringing supplies to England. On the very first day of the attack, Captain John Sirius of the *Iota* sank five great ships, totaling about 50,000 tons, in the English Channel. He gave no warning, torpedoed or gunned down his victims, and fled underwater.

He invaded harbors in France, sinking any and all

ships with cargoes for England. Though she was a neutral, the American ship *Vermondia* was his next victim. The submarine flotilla blockaded London, Southampton, Bristol, Liverpool, all of England's chief harbors. They cut off shipping in the North Channel and the approaches to Glasgow.

Starving England was quickly humbled and brought to her knees. She had been stupidly blind. She had believed that her enemy would abide by the rules of warfare and that enemy submarines would not wantonly attack and destroy unarmed merchant ships. In *Danger* Doyle even described the zigzag tacks ships would have to take in trying to avoid torpedoes fired from submarines lying quiet on the sandy bottom of the sea in wait for their prey. This was just what the German U-boats did in World War I, in which the submarine became Germany's deadliest and most effective naval weapon.

As the military had derided the ideas which Doyle put forward after the Boer War, naval officers now ridiculed his fears of the submarine. Doyle, of course, foresaw correctly in both instances. What he advocated now and fought for in the press was the building of a tunnel, twenty-seven miles long, which would connect England with the European mainland in France. This was described in the House of Commons as an insane idea. The tunnel never materialized. Now it is under serious governmental consideration in England.

Occasionally, as he says in his autobiography, Conan Doyle was clairvoyant; he could see what was to come. He had accurate premonitions of the dangers to be faced.

Yet even he did not realize how close the world was to war and to some of the horrors he had forecast when, with Lady Doyle, he sailed for a triumphal journey across Canada and into the United States in the spring of 1914.

They went first to New York for a week of sightseeing. As a cricketer, Doyle was thrilled by American baseball and even tried his hand at it. To the surprise of a big-league pitcher who threw him a polite blooper, Doyle drilled one out between first and second. As Sherlock Holmes, Doyle visited The Tombs, New York City's prison, and talked with the prisoners. He found one fellow Britisher behind bars there, but not too unhappy about it. At Sing Sing, New York State's prison up the Hudson River, he had himself locked into a seven-by-four-foot cell, then sat in the electric chair. Dr. Watson might want to describe the sensations sometime.

His son, Adrian M. Conan Doyle, has described an incident that took place when the Doyles visited Coney Island. Followed everywhere by insistent newspaper reporters, whom Doyle tried not to find a nuisance despite the exaggerated stories they filed, they tried the various rides and amusements. At Luna Park they entered Coney Island's largest dance hall. The band struck up "God Save the King" and one thousand dancing couples stood at attention to honor one of the most popular Englishmen alive. He was the second most popular Englishman in the United States, says his son; properly, he was preceded by the Prince of Wales.

It was Conan Doyle as historian who looked forward

to, then enjoyed, their trip across Canada. As guests of the Canadian government, the Doyles traveled in the private railroad car of the president of the Grand Trunk Railway. Doyle had long admired the work of the historian Francis Parkman. He had read and reread *The Jesuits in North America in the Seventeenth Century, The Old Régime in Canada,* and the American's other books. To Doyle, Canada was "Parkman land," and he saw the country, from its cities in the east to its western frontiers, not only as it appeared in 1914 but as it had been in the past that, after Parkman, he described in *The Refugees.* Doyle was interested in everything: the prairie, the farmlands, the brush, the tall grain elevators, the towns with all the conveniences of civilization from which he could still see a moose wander past into the wilds. He and Lady Doyle visited Jasper Park, the newest and wildest of the Canadian national parks which he had been formally invited to inspect. On the way back, they spent another three days at Algonquin Park.

Though the public did not yet know it, Sherlock Holmes had preceded Conan Doyle to the United States on this trip. Before he left Windlesham, Doyle had been writing *The Valley of Fear,* a novel involving the great detective with labor gangsterism in the American coalfields. The story opens and closes in Baker Street. It opens with Holmes and Watson engaged in a bit of brisk repartee which, for once, Watson wins.

There is a surprise on the first page. Professor James Moriarty is not dead. He did not perish at the Reichenbach Falls, any more than Sherlock Holmes did, and the archvillain is cleverly at work again. Holmes recognizes his unmistakable hand in a cipher message he is soon able to translate from the pages of *Whitaker's Almanac.*

This message and an urgent summons from Scotland Yard take Holmes and Watson to the ancient Manor House of Birlston in Sussex, a house guarded by moats and a drawbridge. Its owner, John Douglas, has just had his head blown off by what Holmes immediately recognizes as a peculiarly American weapon — a sawed-off shotgun.

The Valley of Fear is really an American story with a framework of Sherlock Holmes and Dr. Watson in London. Most of the black and devilish action takes place in the coalfields of the Vermissa Valley, presumably in western Pennsylvania, and involves an unholy labor organization known as the Scowrers. Operating as a secret society, the Scowrers beat up or murder all those who for one small reason or another have incurred the displeasure of the gangster lords who rule the lodges of the Ancient Order of Freemen.

In secret rituals, members in good standing bind and blindfold satisfactory pledges, then brand them with a white-hot iron. The initiates must then fulfill certain murderous obligations. The American detective William J. Burns had been a visitor at Windlesham and had told Conan Doyle of the diversions of the "Molly Maguires" in the Pennsylvania anthracite regions.

It is against vicious and brutal men, particularly Bodymaster McGinty of Lodge 341, Vermissa, A. O. F., that Conan Doyle pits a resourceful young Pinkerton operative in a story of violence that ends at 221 B, Baker Street.

A larger and more violent conflict than that between Birdy Edwards and Bodymaster McGinty was about to explode.

The Archduke Francis Ferdinand of Austria was assassinated by a Serb, June 28, 1914. War broke out between Serbia and Austria. The Doyles were back in England early in July. Germany, allied with Austria, declared war on Russia August 1; on France, August 3; invaded Belgium August 4 in violation of a treaty underwritten by Great Britain. England declared war on Germany August 4. The bitter war which the United States would enter in 1917 and which would last until November 11, 1918, was on. Over thirty-seven and a half million men would be casualties on both sides. More than eight and a half million would be dead.

From early in 1915 Germany instituted a submarine blockade of the British Isles. Disregarding international law, Germany ordered her submarines to sink at sight and without warning. During the whole of World War I, German U-boats sank 15,953,786 tons of British, Allied, and neutral shipping. Even as his warnings had been disregarded, Conan Doyle's worst fears were realized.

In 1919 Conan Doyle could point out in the preface to an American edition of *Danger* that his warning of unrestricted submarine warfare had been justified and his predictions proved accurate down to the smallest detail. He had approached important governmental bodies and naval men with his pleas for preparedness against such attack. It seemed to Doyle that, as always, politics had been placed before national welfare.

In 1914 Conan Doyle was saying no "I told you so's." He was pushing to get into England's war with Germany just as soon and in as many ways as he could.

9

Fifty-five years old now but big and powerful, Doyle immediately offered his services as a doctor with Great Britain's combat forces. He was rejected. England had other plans for him. Doyle knew what they were, but he wanted quick action. He went home and organized a volunteer military unit in Crowborough. His idea was that every able-bodied man should be trained for the defense of the country.

The Crowborough Volunteers, one hundred and twenty of them, met, chose noncommissioned officers, and, though they had no rifles as yet, began to drill. Doyle notified the British War Office of the action he had taken and wrote *The Times* of London describing the formation of the Volunteers. His idea caught fire. Some twelve hundred villages and towns all over England wrote him asking information about rules and methods so that they could form similar organizations.

War Office action was prompt. Crowborough Company was on parade when an official message came from the military authorities in London ordering all unauthorized military units to disband. Doyle dismissed his men.

Very quickly the Volunteers were reconstituted on a national basis under government regulations. Sir Arthur Conan Doyle was made a member of the committee, headed by Lord Desborough, which commanded England's entire volunteer forces. At the same time he became a private in the first unit organized, the Crowborough Company of the Sixth Royal Sussex Regiment.

The Volunteers, most of them older men, were a home guard army. It was their mission to supplant the Territorials — corresponding to the National Guard in the United States — which were sworn into Britain's regular forces for duty in the war on the European continent. The Volunteers were soon issued rifles and bayonets. Field equipment followed. For the four years of World War I, Sir Arthur Conan Doyle, in the uniform of a Volunteer private, marched and countermarched, shot on the rifle range, and bivouacked on the Sussex Downs with his company. The Volunteers constituted England's last line of defense should Kaiser Wilhelm of Germany succeed where Napoleon Bonaparte of France had failed, and invade the island.

At one review an inspecting staff officer noted Doyle's South African campaign ribbon and commented, with the condescension of officer to enlisted man, that he had seen service before. At attention, eyes straight ahead, Doyle answered, "Yes, sir." When the officer later asked who the big private was and was told he was "Sherlock Holmes," he winced with embarrassment.

As an enlisted man, Conan Doyle took part in grueling cross-country hikes. He helped guard German prisoners. At one point he was a signalman. At another, he was enlisted chief of a machine-gun crew.

This military service was but a small part of Doyle's wartime activities. At the time of the Boer War the authorities had learned from Doyle himself the value of publicity and propaganda in war. They used Conan Doyle now for the best that was in him.

With Lord Birkenhead he wrote "To Arms!", a pamphlet calling all England to action. He wrote appeals on behalf of English prisoners who were ill-used by the enemy. He wrote propaganda directed at Norway, South America, and many times the United States. He was sent to Scotland to write up a new munitions works at Gretna. He was one of the name writers chosen to help keep the population of Britain and the world informed, yet betray no facts that would be of aid or comfort to the enemy.

As after the Boer War he had been England's lone defender and spokesman to the world, Conan Doyle was one of her spokesmen to her own people during the dark days of World War I when the German armies were overrunning Belgium and France, hammering at the gates of Paris, sweeping toward the Channel, and threatening invasion of England herself.

Pamphlets, articles, books by Conan Doyle continued to appear as the German advances were finally stopped and trench warfare between great stalemated armies settled in for the bitter years of ceaseless artillery bombardment, barbed-wire entanglements, sorties "over the top," and the wholesale slaughter of millions of men. The name A. Conan Doyle on what people read was a guarantee of accuracy and good faith. The public knew him not only as the creator of Sherlock Holmes, but also as the fighting champion of causes in which he believed. Doyle might have preferred front-line service caring for the wounded, but the authorities, in this instance at least, used him wisely and effectively to heighten home-front morale and arouse world sympathy for the Allied cause.

Not that Conan Doyle was often in agreement with the authorities. As in Stonyhurst days, he was often at odds with them. The submarine warfare he had foreseen was now a ghastly reality. He could no longer hope to save the ships that were torpedoed and sunk, but something might be done to save the men who were catapulted into the icy seas. Conan Doyle pled for inflatable life rafts on naval ships. When he saw that he could not persuade the Navy to equip its ships with these, he advocated inflatable rubber belts, a kind of World War I "Mae

West." This part of his agitation worked. Inflatable rubber collars and safety waistcoats were issued to the men of the fleet.

Doyle now tried to help save the lives of soldiers as well as sailors. In *The Times* and other powerful newspapers he argued for body armor for the troops, suggesting steel shoulder pads to supplement the steel helmets already issued and possibly another steel shield over the heart. Doyle was a doctor. He knew a man's vulnerable spots. He was a student of medieval warfare and knew the knight's dependence on his armor. Winston Churchill, First Lord of the Admiralty in World War I, just as he was England's fighting Prime Minister during World War II, agreed with Doyle and wrote him so. Churchill was even then working on the development of the tank, a kind of mobile armor, which Britain introduced and used successfully in the latter part of World War I and which the ground forces of all the major combatants used in World War II.

Unofficially, Conan Doyle was making other important contributions to wartime England. Even as the action was under way, he was writing a history of the war. He had dined, he says somewhere in his autobiography, with half the grandees in the land. He knew the generals as well as the politicians who were guiding England. By organizing an extensive correspondence with these general officers, he gathered battle plans and battle results as the engagements took place, slotted the military details he knew so well into place, and gave the public its first full and accurate information about the war as it was being fought. He used diaries, letters, and interviews as well as the reports of the generals to make his work full and detailed.

The first volume, *The British Campaign in France and Flanders*, appeared in 1916. It covered the outbreak of the war, the battles of Mons and Le Cateau, the first battle of the Marne — where the overwhelming Prussian advance was finally halted and the tide of the war turned — the battle of the Aisne, and the first battle of Ypres.

Volume after volume, covering the war from its beginning to the 1918 Armistice, Doyle's work appeared. His six-volume *History of the Great War* was done with no official help but entirely from the reports of the officers and men doing the actual fighting. Doyle knew that he wrote his history well, and discovered after the war's end when official accounts were available that they differed little from his own, which reflected the actual conditions, thoughts, and emotions of people as the fighting was taking place.

Doyle's oldest son, Alleyne Kingsley, entered the army as a private and rose to captain. He was badly wounded — two bullets in the neck — at the Somme, but recovered after a long convalescence. Doyle's daughter, Mary, worked in a munitions plant. His wife was caring for Belgian refugees at Crowborough. As the authorities requested, Doyle was speaking about the war, as well as writing, wherever he was sent.

Then came his long-awaited chance to get to the front. The Italians, who in World War I fought on the side of the Allies, felt they were not getting enough favorable publicity. The Foreign Office asked Doyle to go and write up the Italian-Austrian front. Doyle had his answer ready. He would be glad to go if he could first inspect the British front so that he would have firsthand evidence of the war in that theater to serve in comparing Italy's action against Austria. Permission was readily given and arrangements were speedily made.

Sir Arthur Conan Doyle did not go to France as the correspondent of any one newspaper or magazine or group of publications. He went as a VIP acting for the British government, a literary man whose observations would be read and opinions noted by millions of his readers. Doyle was entitled, when with troops, to wear his uniform as a deputy lieutenant of Surrey. Silver roses, instead of pips and crowns indicative of officer rank, distinguished a uniform that placed him, he says, somewhere between a full colonel and a brigadier or one-star general.

He went to France in the private train compartment of General Sir William Robertson, to whom he dedicated his history of the war. They crossed the English Channel together in the destroyer which had been placed at the general's disposal.

By car and on foot Doyle got to the front-line trenches. He underwent heavy artillery fire as he talked with the troops, saw the dead lying on the ground in "No Man's Land" between the English and the German trenches. To his great joy he met and talked with the colonel serving as assistant adjutant-general of the Twenty-fourth Division. It was his brother Inness, who years before had played with toy soldiers in the consulting room of a struggling young doctor in Southsea. Doyle lunched and dined with generals at their headquarters, returned several times to front-line posts, saw the observation balloons used to direct artillery fire, and watched German and English fighter planes in the dogfights of World War I.

At general headquarters, then at Montreuil, Doyle had lunch — a command performance — with Field Marshal Sir Douglas Haig, commanding all the British forces in France. They had a long talk. When Doyle told the field marshal that his son was in the line, Haig gave orders that brought Kingsley from the front the next day to meet his father. Later that same day Doyle came on his secretary, a big man like himself, who was now a Territorials major serving as administrator of a devastated French town.

All of Doyle's vibrant patriotism was aroused, as was his hatred of the enemy who destroyed cathedral cities as wantonly as they sank unarmed ships. He thrilled to the appearance of badly wounded French veterans and of men of the Scottish Rifles, the Worcesters, the Welsh, and the Scots Fusiliers at a medal presentation in the market square of Bethune. His strong emotions, as well as the record of what he saw, appear in "A Glimpse of the British Army" in *A Visit to Three Fronts*, published in 1916. More of his pride in England rings in the lines of his wartime poems — "The Guards Came Through," "Ypres," "Grousing," "The Volunteer," and others.

After two days in Paris, Doyle found himself in Padua, Italy, undergoing the terrors of a nighttime air raid. He pushed on to Italian Army headquarters, then at Udine. Accompanied by Italian officers, he advanced to the trenches seven miles away. They demurred when later he urged a visit to a dockyard on the Adriatic which had been captured from the Austrians. Doyle found out why on the way there. Austrian guns found the range of their speeding cars and they raced just ahead of the bursting shells.

Doyle interviewed the Italian commander in the Trentino, saw what he could of the Alpine warfare, winced as he passed a spot by the side of the road where eight medical officers had been killed by a single Austrian shell. Wherever he went, mobs of Italian soldiers surrounded him. They had seldom seen a British uniform before. Doyle hoped that the sight of his and the sympathetic account he wrote of the Italian Army in combat helped their morale just as his words would enlighten the British public about their Mediterranean ally. The Foreign Office declared his mission a complete success.

Doyle was hardly off the train in Paris before he learned that Lord Kitchener, England's Secretary of State for War, had been drowned when the battle cruiser which was carrying him to Russia was sunk off the Orkney Islands. Eight hundred men went down with "K," who had organized England's "New Army" of drafted men, just as he had once organized and governed the Sudan. It was a blow to England and to Doyle, who had admired the famous soldier from their first meeting in Egypt.

With Robert Donald, editor of London's *Daily Chronicle*, which had been publishing Doyle's front-line articles, he called on Georges Clemenceau, soon to be wartime Premier of France. Doyle was not impressed with "The Tiger." He found him overly talkative, belligerent, truculent, and volcanic.

The war was very close to Paris. With a journalist, Doyle paid a quick visit to the front near Soissons. Stern staff officers guided them through the trenches. On a later expedition to other parts of the French front, Doyle talked with priests, with young officers, with poilus, and with French general after French general. Doyle admired the dandified dress of the officers, who were as careful of the crease in their trousers or the flare of their spotless breeches amid the mud and squalor of the trenches as in the salons of Paris.

At three different points along the front, as Doyle journeyed from corps to corps of the French Army, he found them firing five or ten shots to one shot from "the Boche." He admired the warlike energy with which the French, who had plentiful supplies, hurled ammunition at their hated Hun foes.

One French general reminded Doyle of the arrogant and fearless Cyrano de Bergerac — of the great beaked nose and the flashing sword — in Rostand's famous play. Another reminded him of Athos and D'Artagnan combined, of Dumas's *The Three Musketeers*. It was this warlike figure who turned hard eyes on him and demanded to know whether or not Sherlock Holmes was fighting with the British Army. Taken aback, Doyle could only stammer in halting French that the great detective was now too old for combat service.

One part of the road that Doyle and Robert Donald traveled was open to enemy artillery fire. As in Italy, their car nearly caught a burst of shrapnel. The German gunner was just a trifle high and to the left. The French general with them shouted to their driver, and they raced ahead of the next shots.

In the Argonne, Doyle met still another type of French officer. This was a heroic and scrappy French-Canadian from a homestead in Alberta. His profanity was picturesque and his patois amusing, but there was no doubt about his bravery. Doyle decided that French officers showed greater individuality than their British counterparts. There was another difference. The British were officers and gentlemen, but gentlemen first. French officers, gentlemanly as they might be, were soldiers first and last.

World War I was not the sporting type of war Doyle had celebrated in so many of his stories. It was a brutal, grueling struggle in holes and ditches, fought not between gallant champions of the knightly caste but between great masses of men, most of them conscripts. It was a muddy, murderous conflict in trenches stretching across Europe for hundreds of miles. It was methodical butchery amid the thunder of constant artillery fire. Attack and counterattack, bombardment and counterbombardment — that was the harsh rhythm. The fledgling air forces alone maintained a kind of bravado and gallantry. Victor saluted vanquished with courtly gestures when fighter planes met in single combat. There were no shining swords and lances, no ladies' tokens in this war. A kind of romance might survive in the air, but this was only icing on an ugly cake.

A generation of Europe's manhood was systematically and painstakingly being blown to bits or ground into the scarred earth. Casualties on both sides were frightful. France suffered the destruction of its cities and monuments, of its countryside as well as its men. The best men of England were bloodily and uselessly expended for four years. There was little that could be glamorized about this war of attrition in which depletion was followed by exhaustion and, each side hoped, would be followed by annihilation of the other.

One suggestion Doyle brought back to England. Wound stripes for the uniform sleeves of men who had suffered but survived would give them some consolation and recognition. The French already used them. The suggestion was adopted.

In April 1917, the month the United States entered the war against Germany, Prime Minister David Lloyd George invited Conan Doyle to breakfast at No. 10 Downing Street.

The two men talked of Kitchener, of the Irish and Welsh Divisions — for Lloyd George was of Welsh as Doyle was of Irish extraction — and of the disastrous Dardanelles campaign in Turkey. The Prime Minister praised Doyle's history of the war. They discussed the use of armor and deplored the revolution which had just occurred in Russia where, Doyle prophesied correctly, a new dictator would arise.

In September 1917 Doyle was on his way to the front again, this time to observe and report on the Australian forces in action in the conflict which now embroiled most of the civilized world. He was present when the American forces, which spearheaded the attack, followed by Australian divisions, smashed through the vaunted Hindenburg Line. Field Marshal Paul von Hindenburg, later Chancellor of Germany, commanded all the German forces in France. The Hindenburg Line was the supposedly impregnable position behind which the Germans were entrenched.

The night before, Doyle had met and talked with Inness, dining with him in the headquarters mess of the Third British Corps. The battle was going on as he started for the front in the morning. He passed ambulances filled with casualties and long lines of walking wounded as he pressed forward in the car assigned him. German whiz-bangs screamed overhead as he tried to talk with a howitzer battery commander and his crew who, for six hours, had been steadily shelling German positions.

At this point Doyle was within one thousand yards of the Hindenburg Line. He got even closer to the battle when an Australian captain volunteered to lead him to a better vantage point. They scrambled forward and, from the top of a disabled tank, watched through their field glasses as the Germans laid down a smoke screen before the advancing Americans and Australians. When searching German shells began to fall uncomfortably close, Doyle and his companion were forced to retreat. On the way to the rear, Doyle's car rounded a corner to come upon a sickening tangle of dead and mutilated men and horses just struck by a German shell.

If Sir Arthur Conan Doyle was at war, so was Sherlock Holmes. Not Conan Doyle but Dr. John W. Watson wrote the preface to *His Last Bow* in 1917. Dr. Watson explained that Sherlock Holmes had been for five years in retirement on a small farm near Eastbourne on the South Downs in Sussex. Like every patriotic Englishman, he had come forward in time of crisis, placing his great and peculiar powers at the disposal of the government as soon as war threatened.

It was, of course, undercover work to which Holmes was assigned. Quickly, Holmes was quietly but surely at work in England's behalf. With the sources at his disposal he had known, of course, how long England's enemies had been plotting against her and the preparations they had been making years before the conflict broke out.

It was November 1895. A dense yellow fog held London. Queen Victoria still ruled the British Empire. Mycroft Holmes, deep in the secret workings of the government, sent an urgent message to his brother. A clerk in the Woolwich Arsenal had been found dead in the Underground, and the plans of the Bruce-Partington submarine were missing.

It was vital that they be recovered. Sir James Walter, charged with responsibility for the plans, died of the shock. Holmes knew as well as he that any nation which obtained the plans could construct the new submarine and use it against England. The country was in grave danger. Watson knew the magnitude of the crime and the extent of the peril when he received a peremptory summons to meet Sherlock Holmes at Goldini's restaurant, Gloucester Road, Kensington, and have with him a burglar's jimmy, a dark lantern, a chisel, and his revolver.

Holmes already knew that the foreign agent behind

the murder and the theft was Hugo Oberstein. Imperturbably, surely, with Watson's loyal help, he moved toward a solution of the mystery, the punishment of the evildoers, and the safety of the Empire.

That Holmes solved one of his most exciting cases and warded off a national disaster is clear, for one day after the conclusion of the case he visited Windsor Palace. He returned to Baker Street with a remarkably fine emerald tiepin. He would say only that it was a gift from "a certain gracious lady" for whom he had been able to do some slight service. Watson and the readers of *The Strand* could easily guess who the gracious lady was.

Watson told all the details that he was free to disclose of Sherlock Holmes's undercover activities, but some of the stories in *His Last Bow* have nothing to do with the war. "The Adventure of Wisteria Lodge," the gruesome "Adventure of the Cardboard Box," and "The Adventure of the Devil's Foot," with its frightening story of the Cornish Horror, are merely fascinating tales of Holmes and Watson steaming themselves in the Turkish bath, as they loved to do, and living the thrillers that end inevitably with Sherlock Holmes triumphant.

The world nearly loses Holmes in "The Adventure of the Dying Detective." Watson himself is nearly paralyzed with fear. He is really too frightened to enjoy one of the funniest passages in all the stories — when the delirious Holmes begs him from what appears to be his deathbed to rearrange the coins in his pockets so that he will be better balanced.

The action of the book's title story takes place on the

eve of England's declaration of war in 1914. Holmes faces a strong and wily antagonist in Von Bork, most dangerous of the Kaiser's secret agents in England. One of the spy's sources is an Irish-American, bitter in his hatred of England, who supplies him with military and naval information about Great Britain. The man's name is Altamont. What Von Bork, who prided himself on the width and depth of his knowledge, did not know was that the father of Sir Arthur Conan Doyle was Charles *Altamont* Doyle. What more natural than that Sherlock Holmes should borrow that name for an alias? This ignorance costs Von Bork dearly. About to flee for Germany with dossiers crammed with misinformation carefully supplied by "Altamont," he learns bitterly as he is led away that his captor is the one man who could have known him and duped him into betrayal of his plans.

Conan Doyle worked vigorously in many ways to maintain public morale, to keep British wartime spirits high despite the heavy casualties in France, at the Dardanelles, and on the high seas, and in the face of air raids and wartime privations at home. His history of the war, his speeches and articles in support of the war effort, his work on behalf of the men of the army and the fleet and British prisoners of war — all were effective. Perhaps it was of equal importance and value that he showed Sherlock Holmes and Dr. Watson still at their accustomed pursuits and gave his readers those familiar figures and the gripping adventures that enabled them to forget for a little while the horrors through which they were living.

Sir Arthur Conan Doyle was seated in the lobby of London's giant Grosvenor Hotel on the day in November 1918 when the war ended with the signing of the Armistice. A well-dressed woman of ordinarily reserved type came through the revolving door from the street and waltzed slowly about with a flag in each hand, then went out without saying a word. Doyle rushed into the street where crowds were shouting, cheering, singing, and waving other flags. In an open car he saw three officers and a tough-looking civilian. The civilian pulled out a bottle of whiskey, tore it open, and drank straight from the bottle. Conan Doyle could have killed him.

With everyone else he rejoiced that the war was over, but it had been a bitter war for him.

His brother-in-law, Dr. Malcolm Leckie, had died of shrapnel wounds while serving at the front. Two nephews, Alec Forbes and Oscar Hornung, had each got bullets through the brain. Lily Loder Symonds, Lady Doyle's closest friend, lived with them as a member of the Doyle family at Windlesham. Three of her brothers had been killed and a fourth wounded. Major Leslie Oldham, the husband of Doyle's sister Lottie, had been killed in the trenches by a sniper.

There was worse. Doyle's son Alleyne Kingsley had recovered from his wounds but been left badly weakened. He died in London of pneumonia. Brigadier General Inness Hay Doyle, worn out by four years of active service, visited England briefly after the Armistice, and then returned to France. He died there of pneumonia.

10

For most of his adult life Sir Arthur Conan Doyle had been interested in spiritualism. Spiritualism is the belief that personality lives on after death and that it is possible for living people to communicate with the spirits of the dead through mediums. Mediums are persons of great sensitiveness who, in trancelike states resembling sleep or deep hypnosis, are believed to receive and transmit messages from departed spirits.

While he was still a young doctor in Southsea, Doyle attended séances. A séance is a meeting of people who are trying through a medium or in other ways to get in touch with the dead. Sometimes spirits manifested their presence through moving the table about which the people were gathered, sometimes by rappings which could not be accounted for by any action of the people present, sometimes by speaking through the voice of the medium.

Conan Doyle was not impressed. Certainly he was not convinced. If anything, he was skeptical. He felt that there were reasonable physical explanations for most of the psychic — that is, spiritual — manifestations he saw and heard.

Yet he was interested, and, as always when he was interested in anything, he began to read all he could find on the subject. This was in 1886. He organized séances himself and sometimes, he says, got surprising results. Doyle joined the Psychical Research Society about 1891. With others who had been appointed as a committee, he investigated the strange noises at a supposedly haunted house. They could find no worldly reason for the strange sounds they heard. Doyle began soon to realize that there was a great deal of evidence for spiritualism that no one — even those who attacked it as a fraud and ridiculed it in books and articles — had ever satisfactorily explained away.

Sir Oliver Lodge, the eminent physicist of University College in Liverpool, was knighted on the same day as Conan Doyle. While they waited for the ceremonies to begin, the two men spent several hours discussing spiritualism. Lodge, a scientist with a scientist's precise mind, was already a convinced and outspoken believer. Doyle continued his studies and investigations. His interest in the occult became so intense that he wrote one short novel about some of those things which are ordinarily beyond the reach of everyday understanding.

In *The Parasites,* 1894, a brilliant young professor of physiology allows himself to be hypnotized by a medium. The medium is a woman from the West Indies, Miss Penclosa. Against his will and despite his utter disbelief in such powers, this lame and unattractive woman victimizes Austin Gilroy through posthypnotic suggestion. He is entirely at her mercy and without a will of his own. The hypnotist makes him fall in love with her. When he rebels, she forces him to make a fool of himself on the lecture platform and wreck his promising university career.

Gilroy suffers all kinds of mental torture as the medium forces him to attack and nearly kill a colleague who had been one of her earlier victims. Even when he locks himself in his room he cannot prevent himself from acting as Miss Penclosa bids. Finally, through her posthypnotic control, the woman makes him try to dash a bottle of acid into the beautiful face of Agatha Marden to whom he is engaged. Doyle gives the story a happier ending, but he paints demoniac possession as possible and does not attempt to explain away the powers of the medium.

World War I sharpened Conan Doyle's interest in spiritualism. As he wrote in *The New Revelation,* 1918, he saw suddenly that spiritualism was not merely the study of forces beyond the ordinary rules of science,

but a force for good. It could break down the walls between life and death and provide messages of hope to
people when they were most deeply afflicted by the loss
of loved ones.

Further study now convinced Conan Doyle of the
validity of spiritualism. Halfway measures never suited
Doyle. Once he was its avowed adherent, he dropped
almost all his other interests to champion the cause of
spiritualism. He had long had a presentiment that his real
career would be not literary but religious. This time the
knightly Conan Doyle, his religious impulses long sup-
pressed, found his crusade. Adrian M. Conan Doyle, who
finds hereditary influences strong in his father, saw it
as influencing this decision. In *The True Conan Doyle*
he says that just as his ancestors had sacrificed all for
their Roman Catholic faith, Conan Doyle now sacrificed
everything for spiritualism.

He bent all the persuasive powers of his pen and his
platform presence to the cause of spiritualism. Book followed book: *The New Revelation*, *The Vital Spirit*,
The Coming of the Fairies, *The Wanderings of a Spiritualist*, *American Adventures*, *Our African Winter*. In
1926, with the help in research of W. Leslie Curnow, he
published a two-volume *History of Spiritualism*, which
he dedicated to Sir Oliver Lodge. Usually Doyle signed
his imaginative works and histories "A. Conan Doyle."
It indicates the seriousness with which he took this work,
which he continued for the rest of his life, that he signed
this history with his full name, his professional and honorary degrees, and the titles of his new responsibilities.

The History of Spiritualism is by Arthur Conan Doyle, M.D., LL.D., President of the London Spiritualist Alliance and President of the British College of Psychic Research.

Conan Doyle was deeply confident of the validity of psychic science and of this work. He considered his history of spiritualism a solid achievement which might some day become the standard text on the subject. He was equally confident that spiritualism itself would eventually be recognized instead of derided, usually by those who had made no serious study of the subject or honest inquiry into it.

Traveling continually, Conan Doyle lectured on spiritualism throughout the far-flung British Empire: Kenya, Rhodesia, Australia, New Zealand, Canada. He spoke in many parts of the United States and across Europe. He spoke only of what, pledging his word of honor, he says in his autobiography he *knew* to be the truth.

In 1927 Conan Doyle published a book that was not about spiritualism at all. He had killed Sherlock Holmes once. He had retired him several times. The title of *His Last Bow* had indicated that this time the great detective's retirement was final. It was not. Editors would not have it so. The public would not have it. No one would have it. The new stories ran first in *The Strand*, then in such magazines as *Collier's*, *Liberty*, and *Hearst's International* in the United States before *The Case Book of Sherlock Holmes* appeared.

Over a period of nearly forty years Sherlock Holmes and Dr. John H. Watson had walked the world of crime and intrigue and lived in their snug lodgings at 221 B, Baker Street in London. Conan Doyle had written four full-length books about them and fifty-six short stories. Now he added a dozen more stories to make the total, books included, seventy-two detective thrillers about the most famous sleuth and the most dauntless doctor-biographer companion that ever were.

Once Conan Doyle had detested Sherlock Holmes enough to push him over the edge of a cliff and be done with him. He had brought him back only when virtually forced to and kept him alive only on sufferance. Over the years Doyle and Holmes had become somewhat reconciled. Holmes, as Doyle knew, could be very charming when he wished. After all, he was as valorous and gallant, as utterly honest, as devoted to his craft as was Doyle himself. Perhaps Doyle had never hated him as much as he thought.

It was just that Sherlock Holmes had taken up too much of the time he wished to devote to other matters, directed too much of his energy into one channel. He had brought him back reluctantly in *The Return*, but Conan Doyle admitted now that he had never regretted the resurrection. Holmes had not prevented his writing history, historical romances, poetry, plays, wartime propaganda, and engaging in psychic research. He had done all of these things and written the Holmes stories as well. Perhaps Sherlock Holmes had interfered a little with critical recognition of what Conan Doyle still considered his more serious work, but that was all. After all the years between 1887 and 1927, Conan Doyle could feel proudly that the last Holmes story was as good as the first, and he was right.

The medieval knight loved to steep his sore muscles and aching joints in water as nearly boiling as he could endure. Perhaps Holmes and Watson had inherited their weakness for this indulgence. They are in the drying room of the familiar Turkish bath again when Holmes, in answer to a question from Watson, shoots a long thin arm out from under the enveloping sheets and draws a letter from the inside pocket of his coat. It is a plea from a titled client to see him about a very important and delicate matter. Holmes almost gets himself murdered before this mystery is solved.

A Derby entry, the bones of a man dead a thousand years, and Holmes all play their separate parts in "The Adventure of Shoscombe Old Place." It was fitting that there should be at least one mystery involving a racehorse, for Watson confessed that he spent about half his wound pension in betting on the races. With seeming seriousness, Holmes makes a confession of a different sort to young Inspector MacKinnon of the Yard in "The Adventure of the Retired Colourman." He admits that he had sometimes considered burglary instead of detection as a profession and felt confident he would have done very well at it. There is little doubt that he would have succeeded admirably.

Many times over the years there had been intimations. Once before there had been almost an avowal of the manly affection between Holmes and Watson. Violence breaks down the barriers of reserve when an American thug and counterfeiter fires point-blank at Watson in the darkened, curio-crammed room in "The Adventure of the Three Garridebs."

Holmes crashes the butt of his revolver down on Killer Evans's head and throws his wiry arms about his companion of forty years.

> "You're not hurt, Watson? For God's sake, say that you are not hurt!"
> It was worth a wound — it was worth many wounds — to know the depth of loyalty and love which lay behind that cold mask. The clear, hard eyes were dimmed for a moment, and the firm lips were shaking. For the one and only time I caught a glimpse of the great heart as well as of a great brain. All my years of humble but single-minded service culminated in that moment of revelation.

Still trembling, Holmes turns on Evans and swears to him that if he had killed Watson he would never have escaped that room alive. It is an emotional passage in one of their last adventures, and one is glad for Watson.

Sir Arthur Conan Doyle wrote to entertain, to interest, and to amuse. Except in his books about spiritualism and when he rose to the defense of England after the Boer War and used his pen as weapon in World War I, he was not out to teach or to convert but to please. He believed it was his chief duty as a writer to leave people a little happier than he found them.

He said this in the preface to the Author's Edition of

his work in 1902 and insisted in that preface that a writer was doing his job only when he interested his readers. Interest was the thing. Interest was his touchstone. The world's great books are all very different from each other. What they have in common is that in one way or another they compel interest. The greatest writers of fiction — and Doyle listed Scott, Thackeray, Dickens, Reade, and Poe — were great because they interested not just a few people but many. A writer may use any treatment he chooses. He may make his book adventurous, poetic, humorous, or whatever else pleases him, but first he must make it interesting.

"It is just this power of holding the attention," Doyle wrote, "which forms the art of story-telling — an art which may be developed and improved but cannot be imitated. It is the power of sympathy, the sense of the dramatic. There is no more capricious and indefinable quality. The professor in his study may have no trace of it, while the Irish nurse in the attic can draw out the very souls of his children with her words. It is imagination — and it is the power of conveying imagination."

By his own standards, Conan Doyle must be counted among the great fiction writers in English. He had imagination, and he made his imagination contagious. He had the power to make men and women forget their own lives and surroundings and live where and when his stories took place and with his characters, whether at 221 B, Baker Street in London with Holmes and Watson, with Brigadier Etienne Gerard during the Napoleonic wars, with Professor Edward Challenger in a lost world of apemen and dinosaurs in South America, or with Sir Nigel Loring in fourteenth-century England.

Conan Doyle was not out to change the world. He propounded no panaceas in his stories. Instead, he was out to describe the world of the past, the world in which he lived, and the imaginary worlds he envisioned in highly colored stories charged with life and filled with dramatic excitement — and that is what he did. He had thrilled to thrillers when he was a boy; he thrilled others with his thrillers throughout his active, varied life.

He knew men of action because he was a man of action. He knew gentlemen like his heroes because he was a gentleman. He knew much about many subjects because his restless curiosity impelled him to find out about them, and all was grist for his storyteller's mill. He was both a highly skilled craftsman and an intelligent man who kept his feet on the ground while he let his imagination soar.

Fully alive himself, he knew how other men who were fully alive lived in the Middle Ages, in the late seventeenth and early nineteenth centuries, and in his own late Victorian, Edwardian, and Georgian times. He quickened his heroes with the same chivalric and knightly ideals which, learned as a boy in Edinburgh, governed his conduct and his attitudes toward other people all his life and were reflected in all his books.

Scott, Macaulay, Poe, and Reade were his literary heroes, as Parkman and one other were his mentors in history. The one other was Edward Gibbon. If he were allowed only one book on a desert island, he said, it would be Gibbon's *Decline and Fall of the Roman Empire*, the history of a thousand years of human life in Europe. He loved George Borrow's tales of gypsy life in England and the organ-roll of Borrow's sentences. For Doyle, writing in the first quarter of the twentieth century, Charles Reade's *The Cloister and the Hearth* and Tolstoy's *War and Peace* were the great novels. Yet it was always the tales of the golden age of knighthood which stirred his blood. Washington Irving's *Conquest of Granada* was such a tale. "I could not name a book," he wrote in 1923, "which gets the beauty and the glamor of it better than this one, the lance-heads gleaming in the dark defiles, the red bale fires glowing on the crags, the stern devotion of the mail-clad Christians, the debonaire and courtly courage of the dashing Moslems."

Bret Harte, Washington Irving, Oliver Wendell Holmes (whom he considered a better essayist than Charles Lamb), Herman Melville, Edgar Allan Poe — American writers always appealed to Conan Doyle. The United States appealed to him always. He felt a sympathy with things American, deplored the war which had separated its North American colonies from England, and insisted on the spiritual unity of the two countries.

In *The Stark-Munro Letters* young Dr. Conan Doyle regretted the misunderstandings which had arisen between "the two great brothers." In "The Adventure of the Noble Bachelor," one of the original *Adventures of Sherlock Holmes* — about twenty-five years before England and the United States were World War I allies and almost a half-century before they were even more closely joined in World War II — Sherlock Holmes says, "... I am one of those who believe that the folly of a monarch and the blundering of a minister in far-gone years will not prevent our children from being some day citizens of the same world-wide country under a flag which shall be a quartering of the Union Jack with the Stars and Stripes."

Every imaginative writer is all of his characters. That is, he imagines them and creates them partly out of what he observes of others but mostly out of what he knows and expresses, sometimes unconsciously, of himself. He cannot help doing this for he is the only person he knows well and confidently. Etienne Gerard, Edward Challenger, Micah Clarke, Alleyne Edricson, and all the others are Conan Doyle, some emphasizing one, some another part of his complete character. Conan Doyle might despise Sherlock Holmes, grow to hate him, then merely to endure him because he had conceived of him originally as being all coldly rational, a mere mechanism of a man with few likable traits and no heart. Try as he might, Doyle could not keep Holmes all mind and represent only his own powers of observation and deduction. His own warmth of heart, humor, and high principles of conduct crept in, and Sherlock Holmes became as real as his maker. Dr. Watson was already warmly human.

Doyle might feel irritation that Holmes interfered with his other work, then interfered with proper appreciation of that work, but he knew something else, too, and said it more than once. Once more, he was talking of other writers when he said it, but again it applies to him. He felt that, in the end, good writing is seldom overlooked, and he said that writing, like water, will always find its true level. Over the long term, the public is seldom wrong in its judgment of a book or any work of art. Millions of readers were never wrong in their delight in Sherlock Holmes and Dr. John H. Watson.

Sir Arthur Conan Doyle wrote stirring historical novels. So did Sir Walter Scott, Robert Louis Stevenson, and, in our own day, Kenneth Roberts. *The White Company*, *Micah Clarke*, and *Sir Nigel* belong in the company of *Quentin Durward*, *Kidnapped*, and *Arundel*. Conan Doyle was a skilled propagandist for England after the Boer War and during World War I. He wrote imaginative science fiction as gripping and as convincing as some of Jules Verne's. In all of these departments of writing he can stand with his peers.

Other men, notably Poe and Gaboriau, had written detective stories before him, but Conan Doyle brought the detective story to a perfection which they did not approach and which detective-story writers since his time, even the best of them, have not been able to come near. In this department, Sir Arthur Conan Doyle is peerless. In plot, action, suspense, drama, humor, and in character he has not been equaled. He is the acknowledged and widely but never successfully imitated master. There is only one Sherlock Holmes — one 221 B, Baker Street — one London of 1895 — and one Conan Doyle.

While on another lecture tour on spiritualism in 1929, Doyle was stricken with a heart attack in Copenhagen, Denmark. He had to be carried ashore from the ship which brought him back to Dover. He was rolled in a Bath chair from the great Victoria Station in London to an apartment which he had kept for many years in nearby Buckingham Palace Mansions.

Despite his serious illness, he insisted on addressing large crowds in Queen's Hall on the morning of Armistice Sunday and another large crowd in Albert Hall that night. The ordeal might have killed him, but it did not. He pulled through this crisis, but a long convalescence at Windlesham followed. There Conan Doyle worked on a new edition of his *Memories and Adventures*, which had first been published six years before. Even when he wrote the new final chapters for the book, he was still living in two rooms of his home to save his strength, and had not yet walked a thousand yards from his door.

He was tired. He felt that he had known many adventures in his seventy-one years. He felt at peace as he waited either for renewed strength to go on with his work or for what he called final rest. He felt that death, when it came, would be the most glorious adventure of all.

Sir Arthur Conan Doyle died at Windlesham in Crowborough, Sussex, on the morning of July 7, 1930.

SIR ARTHUR CONAN DOYLE

1859 — Born May 22 in Edinburgh, Scotland.

1869 — Entered Hodder House.

1871 — Entered Jesuit public school, Stonyhurst, in Lancashire, England.

1875 — Attended Jesuit school in Austria.

1879 — Wrote first published story, "The Mystery of Sasassa Valley."

1880 — Sailed Arctic aboard whaler *Hope.*

1881 — Graduated from the University of Edinburgh as a Bachelor of Medicine and Master of Surgery. Sailed to West Africa aboard the *Mayumba.*

1882 — Began the practice of medicine in Southsea, Portsmouth.

1885 — Married Louise Hawkins.

1887 — *A Study in Scarlet.*

1889 — *Micah Clarke.*

1890 — *The Sign of the Four.*

1891 — *The White Company.*
Studied in Vienna.
Began practice in London as an oculist.
Abandoned medicine as a profession.

1893 — *Adventures of Sherlock Holmes.*
Residence in Switzerland.

1894 — Lecture tour in the United States.
Memoirs of Sherlock Holmes.

1895 — *The Stark-Munro Letters.*

1896 — War correspondent in the Egyptian Sudan.
Built "Undershaws," Hindhead, Surrey.
The Exploits of Brigadier Gerard.
1900 — Served with the Langman Hospital in South
Africa, Boer War.
The Great Boer War.
1901 — Defeated for Parliament.
1902 — August 9, knighted by Edward VII for services
to England.
The Hound of the Baskervilles.
1905 — Again defeated for Parliament.
The Return of Sherlock Holmes.
1906 — *Sir Nigel.*
Louise Hawkins Doyle died.
Defended George Edalji.
1907 — September 18, married Jean Leckie.
Bought "Windlesham," Crowborough, Sussex.
1912 — *The Lost World.*
1914 — Visited Canada and the United States.
1914–1918 — Served four years as a private of Volunteers;
visited British, French, Italian, and Australian
fronts: *The British Campaign in France and
Flanders, A Visit to Three Fronts,* etc.
The Valley of Fear, 1915.
His Last Bow, 1917.
1918 — *The New Revelation.*
1926 — *The History of Spiritualism.*
1927 — *The Case Book of Sherlock Holmes.*
1930 — July 7, died at Windlesham.

BIBLIOGRAPHICAL NOTE

Chief source for this book has been the voluminous and varied writings of Sir Arthur Conan Doyle: his novels and short stories, histories, miscellaneous prose writings; and particularly his *Memories and Adventures*, 1924 and 1930, and the autobiographical *Stark-Munro Letters*, 1895.

The standard biography is *The Life of Sir Arthur Conan Doyle*, 1949, which was written, with access to Conan Doyle's notes and letters and with the assistance of the Conan Doyle family, by John Dickson Carr. Conan Doyle's son, Adrian M. Conan Doyle, published *The True Conan Doyle* in 1945. This was in part an answer to Hesketh Pearson's *Conan Doyle*, 1943, which was not published in the United States until 1961.

There are a score of books about Sherlock Holmes and Dr. John H. Watson. Some of these are informative and a few are amusing. All of them certify to the fascination which Conan Doyle's most famous characters exert on organized groups of their admirers, the Baker Street Irregulars in the United States and the Sherlock Holmes Society in England. They appeal as well to the unorganized multitudes who are almost equally fanatical in their devotion to "the world's first consulting detective" and his intrepid companion.

Most of these books gravely assume that Holmes and Watson were living men. Generally they either ignore Conan Doyle, grant him nominal attention, or with gentle facetiousness refer to him as someone whom Sherlock Holmes and Dr. Watson knew rather casually. Greater tribute could hardly be paid Sir Arthur Conan Doyle as an imaginative writer than this acceptance of his creations as having independent lives of their own.